ANCIENT ROME

INFANTRY
SWORD

ROMAN
COIN

LEATHER
HORSE MASK

WALL MOSAIC

P · O · C · K · E · T · S

ANCIENT ROME

Written by
SUSAN McKEEVER

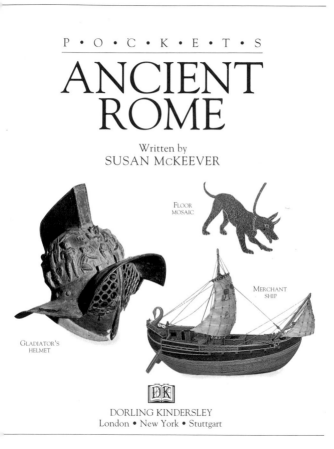

FLOOR
MOSAIC

MERCHANT
SHIP

GLADIATOR'S
HELMET

DK

DORLING KINDERSLEY
London • New York • Stuttgart

A DORLING KINDERSLEY BOOK

Project editor Linda White
Art editor Sarah Ponder
Senior editor Laura Buller
Senior art editor Helen Senior
Production Catherine Semark
Louise Barratt
Editorial consultant Simon James
Picture research Christine Rista

First published in Great Britain in 1995
by Dorling Kindersley Limited
9 Henrietta Street, Covent Garden, London WC2E 8PS

2 4 6 8 10 9 7 5 3

Copyright © 1995 Dorling Kindersley Ltd., London

Visit us on the World Wide Web at http://www.dk.com

A CIP catalogue record for this book is available from
the British Library.

ISBN 0 7513 5183 0

Colour reproduction by Colourscan, Singapore
Printed and bound in Italy by L.E.G.O.

CONTENTS

How to use this book

These pages show you how to use *Pockets: Ancient Rome*. The book is divided into a number of sections, which cover different aspects of ancient Roman life. At the back of the book is a useful reference section. Each new section begins with a page that lists its contents.

ROMAN LIFE
Ancient Rome has been divided into subject areas and arranged in eight sections, beginning with "Introduction to ancient Rome", which sets the scene by providing an overview of the subject and a brief history.

Corner coding

Heading

Introduction

GAMES AND LEISURE

THE THEATRE

THEATRE RUINS
The Romans built theatres all over the empire, like this theatre of Aspendus in Asia Minor.

THE ROMANS adopted the i of theatre from the Greeks. first, translations of Greek were performed. Later, orig plays were written by Rom playwrights such as Plautus and Terence. Comedies were preferred to tragedies. Mime was a Roman invention, but, unlike today's mime, actors spoke!

IN THE WINGS
In this mosaic a group of actors are preparing for a play. Two actors are practising dance steps, one actor is being helped into his costume, and a musician is playing double pipes. Masks lie ready to be worn at the performance.

Poorer people sat higher up.

Underneath the seat network of corridor stairs allowed acce

Caption

CORNER CODING
Corners of the main section pages are colour coded to remind you which section you are in.

HEADING
This describes the subject of the page. This page is about the theatre. If a subject continues over several pages, then the same heading applies.

CAPTIONS AND ANNOTATIONS
Each illustration has a caption. Annotations, in *italics*, point out features of an illustration and usually have leader lines.

- ■ INTRODUCTION TO ANCIENT ROME
- ■ ROMAN SOCIETY
- ■ LIFE IN ROME
- ■ THE ROMAN ARMY
- ■ BUILDING AND TECHNOLOGY
- ■ GAMES AND LEISURE
- ■ RELIGION, FESTIVALS, AND DEATH
- ■ THE END OF AN ERA

INTRODUCTION
This provides a clear, general overview of the subject. After reading the introduction, you should have a good idea what the pages are about.

RUNNING HEADS

These remind you which section you are in. The top of the left-hand page gives the section name. The right-hand page gives the subject. Here, The Theatre is in the Games and Leisure section.

FEATURE BOXES

Throughout the book, feature boxes supply extra information about aspects of Roman life, such as types of gladiator. The feature box on this page gives details about Roman theatre masks.

FACT BOXES

The introductory pages to each of the eight sections have fact boxes. These contain interesting facts about the subject covered in that section.

Running head

Feature box

ARCHITECTURE

MUCH OF ROMAN ARCHITECTURE was influenced by the Greeks, but the Romans did make innovations of their own. Massive arched aqueducts brought water to daily life was centred around of the forum, or town square.

MASKS
Theatres were very big, so actors wore masks to help the audience recognize the various types of characters. Masks could indicate happy and tragic figures, male and female, and young and old. Male characters wore brown masks; female wore white. Special devices were built into the masks to help the actors project their voices.

THEATRE PLAN
Roman theatre design followed that of the Greeks, with some changes. Both had a D-shape, with tiers of seats. But Greek seats in Roman theatres were often formed by arches and vaults, rather than being cut into the slope of a hillside. The first wooden theatres were later replaced by sturdier ones of stone.

ARCHES
The use of the arch is a fundamental feature of Roman architecture. The Greeks and the Etruscans also built arches but did not use them in as many different ways. Before the Romans, most buildings were supported by columns and walls. Roman architects were able to build some greater distances because arches can support much heavier loads.

AQUEDUCTS
These consisted of a series of arches on several levels. The water channel at the top maintained a constant gradient.

THEATRE
The raised seating in Roman theatres was supported by arches. The Greeks built their theatres on natural slopes.

BRIDGES
Arched bridges could stretch across rivers and valleys. The falls on either side acted as buttresses, or supports.

TRIUMPHAL ARCH
This type of arch had no practical function. The Romans built triumphal arches to celebrate victory in battle.

AMPHITHEATRES
Tiered arches supported the rows of seating, which completely encircled the amphitheatre's central arena.

The scenery background on the stage was elaborately decorated.

A curtain, or *velarium* could be pulled over these poles to keep the rain off the audience.

The orchestra was the area situated in front of the stage.

The scenery could be changed using special machinery.

velarium fell to reveal the stage.

Arches supported the seats.

Hoists that lifted actors from the stage, trapdoors, and other tricks provided special effects.

Annotation

REFERENCE SECTION

The reference section pages are yellow and appear at the back of the book. On these, you will find useful facts, dates, and charts. This section includes a map showing the expansion of the Roman empire, a list of the Roman emperors, and a feature on Roman architecture.

LABELS

For extra clarity, some pictures have labels. They may give extra information, or identify a picture when it is not obvious from the text what the picture actually is.

GLOSSARY AND INDEX

There is a glossary and an index at the back of the book. The glossary defines and explains words and terms in this book that are specific to ancient Roman life. The index lists every subject alphabetically.

INTRODUCTION TO ANCIENT ROME

WHERE WAS ANCIENT ROME?

THE CIVILIZATION WE KNOW as ancient Rome began nearly three thousand years ago in Rome, now the capital city of Italy. Although Rome gave its name to the civilization, the city was only a small part of the Roman empire, which grew over the centuries to become one of the largest the world has ever known. But the city of Rome remained its centre, and all roads in the empire eventually led there.

ROMA COIN
The goddess Roma was worshipped as the personification of the city of Rome.

FACTS ABOUT ROME

• The history of Rome can be divided into three periods: the rule of kings (c.753-509 B.C.), the Republic (c.509-31 B.C.), and the Empire, when the Roman empire was ruled by emperors (c.31 B.C.-A.D. 476).

• Senators served in the Senate for life.

• In 46 B.C. Julius Caesar established the calendar still basically used today. To do this he added an extra 67 days to 45 B.C.

THE CITY OF ROME TODAY
Today, millions of tourists flock to Rome to visit its many attractions. Thanks to the building skills of the Romans, people can still see temples, statues, monuments, and arches that were built in the days of the empire.

River Tiber

Ponte Sant'Angelo

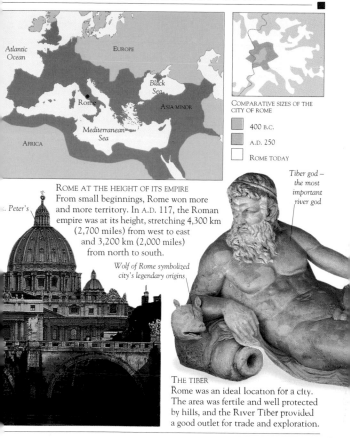

COMPARATIVE SIZES OF THE
CITY OF ROME

- 400 B.C.
- A.D. 250
- ROME TODAY

ROME AT THE HEIGHT OF ITS EMPIRE

From small beginnings, Rome won more and more territory. In A.D. 117, the Roman empire was at its height, stretching 4,300 km (2,700 miles) from west to east and 3,200 km (2,000 miles) from north to south.

Wolf of Rome symbolized city's legendary origins

Tiber god – the most important river god

THE TIBER

Rome was an ideal location for a city. The area was fertile and well protected by hills, and the River Tiber provided a good outlet for trade and exploration.

THE SOURCES

OUR KNOWLEDGE of ancient Rome comes from the variety of artefacts that remain from Roman times. The Romans left behind buildings, art, and everyday items. Writings by people of the time have also survived – these tell about daily life, politics, and history. Monks in medieval times transcribed the original writings.

MOSAIC
Artists' work, such as this mosaic depicting a Roman birdbath, provides valuable information about the times in which the artist lived.

HORSE MASK
Objects ranging from po[...] and pans to jewellery an[...] shoes have been found on Roman sites. This is a replica of a leather mask found in Britain.

RECONSTRUCTION
With only scant remains, archaeologists can create a remarkably clear picture of people from the past. From a skull, archaeologists are able to build up the musculature over the existing bone structure, until a facial shape of the deceased person emerges.

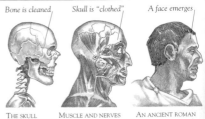

Bone is cleaned

Skull is "clothed"

A face emerges

THE SKULL

MUSCLE AND NERVES

AN ANCIENT ROMAN

Marcus Agrippa
built the original
Pantheon.

M·AGRIPPA·L·F·COS·TERTIVM·FECIT

STONE INSCRIPTIONS

The Romans made inscriptions
on many of their buildings.
The information
is accessible
because these
inscriptions were
written in Latin.

THE BUILDINGS OF ANCIENT ROME

Many Roman buildings have survived almost unchanged.
They reveal architectural styles, building materials, and
town planning. The location of the
buildings also shows the extent
of the empire. These ruins are
from a huge *villa* that emperor
Hadrian built near Rome.

ROMAN COIN
Coins are valuable sources.
They often feature names
and important events.

*Part of the villa's
island sanctuary*

EARLY ROME

BEFORE ROME'S RISE to power, the land of Italy was occupied by a variety of settlers. Among them were Greeks, Etruscans, Samnites, Latins, Sabines and Umbrians. The Latins, who lived on the Latium plains by the River Tiber, were natives of early Rome. Over a period of time, they conquered all the other peoples who were sharing Italy with them.

ETRUSCAN WARRIOR

Etruscans and Greeks

A long time before Romulus's legendary founding of Rome, the Etruscans lived in Etruria, north of the city. They also had settlements in the south. The Etruscans had a thriving civilization based on trade and agriculture. The Greeks colonized areas in southern Italy and Sicily, where they built many fine houses and temples. Both the Greeks and Etruscans had a huge effect on early Rome in terms of art, architecture, religion, and technology.

ETRUSCAN VOTIVE OFFERING

MAP OF PRE-ROMAN ITALY
Pre-Roman Italy was a land of many different cultures and languages. The Sabines living to the north of Rome and the Samnites, who lived in central Italy, were both part of the Otto-Umbrian tribes. All these peoples influenced Roman culture as Rome began to expand.

- ■ GREEK
- ■ LATIN
- ■ OTTO-UMBRIAN
- ■ ETRUSCAN

SARCOPHAGUS FOR HUSBAND AND WIFE
Etruscans believed in life after death.
The dead were buried with jewellery,
artefacts, and food for the next life.
Wealthy people could afford to have
elaborate underground tombs. This
6th-century-B.C. sarcophagus shows
a dead couple feasting at a banquet.

Terracotta coffin

This intricate painting depicts figures from Greek mythology.

GRECIAN URN
The Greeks were
skilled artists.
They produced
exquisite pottery,
metalwork, and
sculptures. Greek
pottery was very
popular in Rome.

Samnite gladiator

Long shield

SAMNITE WARRIOR
The Romans copied their
long rectangular shields
from Samnite warriors.
One type of gladiator
dressed as a Samnite.

This urn is from the 4th century B.C.

Facts and fiction

Legend claims that Rome was
founded in 753 B.C. by twins
called Romulus and Remus.
Although no one knows if this
story is true, it is certain that
the site of the future city was
being settled by farmers at
about this time. This small
community on the seven hills
surrounding the River Tiber
grew over time into the city
of Rome. For more than 200
years, the city was ruled by
kings. The monarchy was later
ousted in favour of a republic.

MARS, GOD OF WAR
Legend says that
Mars, the god
of war, was the
father of Romulus
and Remus. Their
mother was King
Numitor's daughter

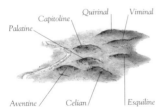

THE SEVEN HILLS OF ROME
Tribes of Latins lived on the seven hills
of Rome, making a living by farming.
They defended their hilltop settlements
from other tribes that lived nearby.
The marshy valley in the middle was
later to become the site of the forum.

Palatine
Capitoline
Quirinal
Viminal
Aventine
Celian
Esquiline

AENEAS THE TROJAN WARRIOR
After his city was destroyed by the Greek
Aeneas founded a new "Troy" in Italy.
Many years later, King Numitor, Aeneas
descendant, was driven out of his city by
his wicked brother, Amulius. When
Numitor's daughter gave birth to twin
sons, Amulius feared a threat to his power

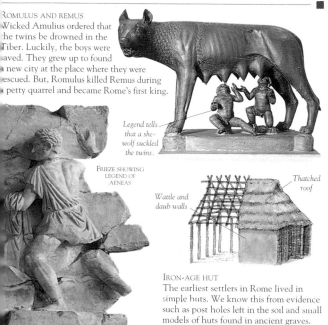

ROMULUS AND REMUS

Wicked Amulius ordered that the twins be drowned in the Tiber. Luckily, the boys were saved. They grew up to found a new city at the place where they were rescued. But, Romulus killed Remus during a petty quarrel and became Rome's first king.

Legend tells that a she-wolf suckled the twins.

FRIEZE SHOWING LEGEND OF AENEAS

Thatched roof

Wattle and daub walls

IRON-AGE HUT

The earliest settlers in Rome lived in simple huts. We know this from evidence such as post holes left in the soil and small models of huts found in ancient graves.

Tarquinius Superbus (Tarquin the Proud) is said to have been a cruel king.

RENAISSANCE PAINTING DEPICTING FOUNDING OF TEMPLE OF JUPITER

THE LAST KING

Following the reign of Romulus, Latin, Sabine, and finally a line of Etruscan kings ruled Rome until 509 B.C. The last king of Rome, Tarquin the Proud, was a tyrant, so the people drove him out and set up a republic.

THE REPUBLIC

IN THE ROMAN REPUBLIC, the power lay not with one person but with a group of people called senators, who met together in the Senate. Every year, Roman citizens voted to select certain senators to be government officials. All senators came from wealthy Roman families. As the majority of citizens were poor, they often felt badly represented by the government.

THE SENATE HOUSE
This building in Rome is a reconstruction of the Senate house, where a council of powerful men met to make decisions about government policy.

Atlas was one of many gods worshipped by Romans.

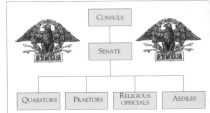

STRUCTURE OF THE ROMAN REPUBLIC
Elected from the Senate were *consuls*, *quaestors*, *aediles*, *praetors*, and religious officials. There were also *censors*, who revised Senate membership and issued contracts for temples and roads. The initials *SPQR*, meaning "the Senate and people of Rome", were put on buildings, army standards, and coins.

RELIGIOUS OFFICIALS
These men supervised public worship of the state gods and looked after sacrifices and festivals. Top official was the *pontifex maximus*, a position later held by the emperor.

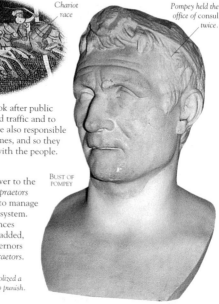

Chariot race

Pompey held the office of consul twice.

AEDILES

Four *aediles* held office to look after public buildings, sewers, streets, and traffic and to provide markets. *Aediles* were also responsible for putting on the public games, and so they often became very popular with the people.

PRAETORS

Second in power to the *consuls*, eight *praetors* were elected to manage Rome's legal system. When provinces abroad were added, provincial governors also acted as *praetors*.

Axe and rods symbolized a praetor's authority to punish.

BUST OF POMPEY

QUAESTORS AND PROCURATORS

These officials were in charge of Rome's finances. As Rome grew in size, they increased in number. This was the official brand of the *procurator* of Britain. He used to collect taxes and pay the army.

CONSULS

Every year, two *consuls* were elected. These men were the most senior officials in the government and were advised by the Senate. To avoid tyranny, each *consul* had the power to veto (stop) the other. So, both had to agree on a decision. In times of trouble, the Senate could elect a *dictator*, who had absolute power.

JULIUS CAESAR

IN REPUBLICAN ROME, a number of generals became very powerful. One of these was Julius Caesar. After serving in a number of government positions, he was elected *consul* in 59 B.C. Caesar's army won large territories for Rome, but his power worried the Senate, and they ordered him to give up his army. He refused, marched on Rome, and seized power as dictator.

CAESAR, THE FIRST LIVING ROMAN TO APPEAR ON A COIN

This relief of Cleopatra is from the temple of Hathor in Egypt.

DATELINE

100 B.C. Born in Rome.

59 B.C. Elected *consul.*

58 B.C. Begins successful Gaul campaign.

55 B.C. Invades Britain.

49 B.C. Marches on Rome and seizes power.

48 B.C. Defeats Pompey.

44 B.C. Declared dictator for life.

44 B.C. Murdered by a group of senators.

CLEOPATRA
Caesar's defiance of the Senate led to civil war. He fought battles all over the empire. During his time in Egypt, Caesar and Queen Cleopatra became lovers and she bore him a son.

CAESAR'S CONQUESTS
Africa Nova in North Africa was added to the empire by Caesar, but his most significant conquest was Gaul (France, Switzerland, Belgium, and part of Germany). This painting shows the proud Gallic leader, Vercingetorix, about to surrender to Caesar.

INVASION OF BRITAIN
Not all of Caesar's campaigns were successful. His attempts to invade Britain were thwarted by the Britons' fierce resistance.

British warriors wore twisted necklaces called tores.

BUST OF CAESAR
Julius Caesar had an aristocratic upbringing. He was a great orator and became very popular with the common people.

DEATH OF CAESAR
This coin commemorates the murder of Julius Caesar. It gives the date, the "ides" (or 15th) of March, and shows two daggers, the murder weapons.

EID · MAR

THE EMPIRE

AFTER CAESAR'S DEATH, civil wars raged until only two men remained in the struggle for power: former *consul* Mark Antony and Caesar's adopted son Octavian. Antony ruled in the East, and Octavian ruled the West. But conflict between the two led to war. After a huge sea battle at Actium in 31 B.C., Octavian emerged as Rome's sole ruler.

LAUREL LEAVES
Emperors wore wreaths of laurel leaves instead of crowns. Laurel crowns had originally been worn by generals to celebrate their military victories.

The first emperor

Octavian was renamed Augustus, meaning "majestic". After the turmoil of civil war, the Roman people were desperate for a strong ruler. Augustus was very careful to keep the idea of the Republic alive and said he was simply "first citizen", one of the people. But he was in fact the first emperor – the Republic was dead and the period of Rome's history known as the Empire had begun.

DATELINE
63 B.C. Born in Rome.
31 B.C. Defeats Mark Antony at Actium.
29 B.C. Declares peace throughout the Roman world.
27 B.C. Given the name "Augustus".
A.D. 14 Dies. Senate declares him a god.

BUST OF AUGUSTUS
A patron of the arts, Augustus was thought to be very handsome

2 4

*Frieze shows
members of the
emperor's family*

Altar

LIVIA

Livia was the wife of Augustus for 53 years and exerted great influence over him.

COIN

This is one of the coins Antony struck to pay his troops during the power struggle with Augustus.

Roman warship

PEACE

Following all the civil wars, Augustus declared peace throughout the Roman world. This monument was built to celebrate the Augustan peace.

BUILDING WORK

Augustus boasted, "I found Rome built of bricks. I leave her covered in marble". He carried out much restoration work on existing buildings and erected a new forum.

Ruins of Augustus's forum in Rome

The emperors

Rome continued to be ruled by emperors for centuries after the death of Augustus. However, they did not all rule wisely. Some seem to have been mad; others were corrupt. At first, there were dynasties whereby emperors were succeeded by members of their family. Later, the army influenced who came to power, and successful generals were often declared emperor by their troops. By the 2nd century A.D., there were emperors from the provinces.

MUREX SHELL

NERO (RULED A.D. 54-68)

Nero was only 16 when he came to power. At first he did what the Senate asked. Later, he became tyrannical. He had his stepbrother, mother, and wife murdered. It is said that he set fire to Rome to build his palace.

Nero erected a colossal statue of himself in Rome.

PURPLE DYE

Purple was the colour usually worn by emperors (for anyone else to dress entirely in purple was treason). The dye was distilled from murex seashells.

Tiberius

Portrait of emperor

CALIGULA (A.D. 37-41)

Said to be mad, Caligula took his horse into the Senate and tried to have it elected as *consul*. He was cruel and unpredictable. The Praetorian Guard finally murdered him.

An illness left Caligula deranged.

TRAJAN (A.D. 98-117)

This arch was built in honour of Trajan, an emperor from Spain. When he conquered Dacia, the empire reached its largest. In Rome, he built Trajan's Markets, a huge complex of shops and offices.

MARCUS AURELIUS (A.D. 161-180)

This benevolent ruler encouraged rich citizens to donate money to the poor. This column commemorates his successful defence of the empire against the barbarian invaders.

Legion's standard

TIBERIUS (A.D. 14-37)

This scabbard has pictures of Tiberius. He ruled well at first, but he became terrified of plots to kill him and forced many people to commit suicide.

ROMAN SOCIETY

ABOUT ROMAN SOCIETY

THE PEOPLE OF ROME fell neatly into two groups: citizens and non-citizens. To be born a citizen brought many advantages, because a non-citizen was denied certain rights. Roman citizens were divided into three classes, according to wealth. Non-citizens were either provincials or slaves. A woman's position in Roman society depended on the status of her husband.

ROMAN FAMILIES
The *paterfamilias*, or father, was all-powerful. He was in charge of his wife and children, the slaves, and all the possessions in the house.

Tunic and cloak

ROMAN CITIZEN
(2ND-CENTURY-A.D. STATUE)

BECOMING A CITIZEN
A boy had a "growing up" ceremony at the age of 14. He gave up his *bulla* (a charm worn around the neck) and became a registered citizen.

PROVINCIALS
The Romans conquered many lands outside Italy. People living in these lands were provincials. This plaque comes from a province in North Africa.

WOMEN IN SOCIETY

Roman women were not educated to a high standard and they could not vote or hold any government position. Married women spent their time engaged in household tasks; the wealthy had slaves to help them. Widows were able to control their own property.

The groom holds a written contract of marriage.

Clasped hands symbolize union of couple and their families

ETTING MARRIED

ost marriages were ranged for financial political reasons. e wedding usually ok place at the ide's house and s witnessed by mily and friends. e bride wore a ecial dress and a ght orange veil.

SLAVES

THE LOWEST RANK in Roman society
was that of slave. Slaves had no legal
rights; they were owned by Romans
who put them to work in their home
and fields. People became slaves when
the Romans conquered their lands
and took them prisoner. Any children
they had were then born into slavery.
Many slaves were treated
very badly, but others
were granted their
freedom. Educated
Greek slaves were
highly prized and
often worked
as doctors
and tutors.

EDUCATED SLAVES
Many slaves were well
educated and artistic.
Musicians, dancers,
actors, and teachers
were usually slaves.

Prisoners
of war

SPOILS OF WAR
Prisoners captured in war
were taken to slave markets
and auctioned off to the
public. A slave became
the property of the highest
bidder. This detail from
Trajan's Column shows a
group of captured Dacians
destined for the slave market

FREEDMEN

Slaves could be freed by their masters or save up to buy their freedom. Known as freedmen, they were not full citizens, but they had more rights than slaves and often owned businesses. This relief marks the tomb of a group of freedmen.

FIGHTING FOR FREEDOM

Gladiators, who were usually slaves, had the chance to win their freedom by success in the arena. A wooden sword was presented the gladiator to signify his freedom.

Gladiator's shield

Slave styles mistress' hair

TENDING THE RICH

ealthy households had several ves responsible for various tasks h as cleaning and cooking. This ture shows the mistress of the house ing her hair done by two slaves.

CITIZENS

ROMAN CITIZENS had certain rights and duties that did not apply to non-citizens. Citizens could vote in the yearly elections, work in government, and be entertained at the public games – but they also had to pay taxes. Citizenship was restricted to people born of free (non-slave) parents, at first in Rome, but later throughout Italy. In A.D. 212 an edict extended these rights to the entire Roman empire.

Shoulder plate

Flexible metal strips

Only legionaries were issued with this highly protective armour.

Woollen tunic

CORN DOLE
Citizens of Rome were entitled to an allowance of free corn, which was made into bread and distributed as loaves. By A.D. 14 some 300,000 people were on the dole.

JOINING THE ARMY
Only citizens could have a decent career in the army. Non-citizens could not be legionaries, the backbone of the army, but they could be auxiliaries. Provincials who joined these support forces were rewarded with citizenship at the end of service.

RANKS OF CITIZENS

The three orders of citizens were senators, equestrians (descendants of the first cavalry officers), and the people. All citizens wore togas on formal occasions; a senator's toga had wide purple borders.

GAMES

All citizens could go to the games. The expression "bread and circuses" describes the free bread and lavish games the government put on to keep the people happy.

This emperor was a powerful military leader.

FIRST CITIZEN

When Augustus became the first emperor, he knew people would be worried that Rome was returning to the rule of kings, so he called himself *princeps*, or "first citizen". After him, all emperors were regarded as first citizens.

SEPTIMIUS SEVERUS
(EMPEROR FROM
A.D. 193-211)

PROVINCIALS

THE MAJOR PART of the vast Roman empire was the provinces. These were lands that the Romans had conquered. Although some subject peoples were already citizens – often by completing service in the Roman army – in A.D. 212 the emperor Caracalla extended citizenship to all provincials. This enabled him to tax more people.

GOVERNOR'S CHAIR
To look after the various provinces, the emperor appointed governors. They sat on special chairs, like the one shown here.

Spain and North Africa

Spain quickly became Romanized after its occupation. Its oldest town, Italica, produced two emperors: Trajan and Hadrian. Spain had mines supplying precious metals. It also exported olive oil, wine, and fish sauce. Africa was first occupied in 146 B.C. after the wars with Carthage. It was a rich province, supplying many types of wild animals for the arena, as well as purple dye, olive oil, and corn.

PROVINCES OF THE ROMAN EMPIRE
This map depicts the Roman empire at its greatest extent. The darker area shows the Roman provinces of Spain and North Africa.

SPAIN

NORTH AFRICA

EMPIRE AT ITS HEIGHT

SPAIN AND NORTH AFRICA

SILVER GOBLET
Spain's precious metals were used to make vessels like this goblet as well as exquisite jewellery.

Many thousands of wild animals perished in Rome's arenas.

WILD ANIMAL TRADE
The town of Leptis Magna in Africa specialized in the trade of wild animals and became very wealthy, spending lavishly to erect magnificent buildings.

Musical instruments

PROVINCIAL-STYLE VILLA
The provinces retained their own architectural styles, but there were also buildings just like those in Rome. Some buildings were a mixture of Roman and provincial styles. The fortifications on this North African *villa* were for defence against attack.

MOSAIC OF A LEOPARD

Look-out tower

Second storey

Enclosed ground floor

Gaul, Britain, Greece, and Danube lands

Gaul and Germany were home to the Celts. The south was more urban, while the north and west were mainly agricultural. Fine crafts and jewellery were made here. Britain, a rich province, provided many goods. Greece was a thriving civilization that greatly influenced Rome. The Danube provinces had many military forts and supplied soldiers for the army.

MARBLE
Rome used marble from Greece in many of its finest buildings.

PORTA NIGRA
Augustus created a flourishing city at Trier, northeast Gaul (now Germany). The Porta Nigra ("black gate") was later added to protect against barbarian invasions.

EMPIRE AT ITS HEIGHT

GAUL, BRITAIN, GREECE, DANUBE

PROVINCIAL MAP
When Dacia (modern Romania) fell to Rome in A.D. 106, the Roman empire was at its biggest.

DOG BROOCH
Exports from Gaul included pottery, hunting dogs, and intricate jewellery such as this bronze brooch.

DACIA
Trajan's Column was built to commemorate the emperor's conquest of Dacia. This detail shows a river god watching Roman troops cross the Danube.

Tiers of arched windows

Face skilfully wrought from iron

IRON MASK
Britain had a large army presence. In peacetime, soldiers would take part in cavalry sports for fun. They wore masks such as this one and fought mock battles on horseback.

VIENNE (FRANCE)
During Roman times, this Gaulish city grew rich due to its surrounding agricultural land. Public buildings, such as this fine temple, can still be seen today.

Egypt and the East

Alexandria, the capital of Egypt and an important cultural centre, was the second largest city in the Roman empire. Most of the corn that fed the empire came from Egypt and was shipped from Alexandria. The province also supplied papyrus for writing, flax, olives, and dates. The eastern provinces exported exotic goods such as silks, spices, dyes, and perfumes. Camel trains carried goods from as far away as India and China to one of the coastal ports for export.

PALMYRA
Trade links with the East made this Syrian city very prosperous.

SWEET-SMELLING THINGS
Perfumes, spices, and flowers came to Rome from the East. This painting shows a woman pouring perfume into a phial.

EMPIRE AT ITS HEIGHT

EGYPT AND THE EAST

Alexandria

EGYPT

PROVINCIAL MAP
Egypt became Roman in 30 B.C. The eastern provinces had all been added by the early 2nd century A.D.

SCENE FROM THE RIVER NILE

Alexandria was a centre of art in the 1st century
B.C., producing many frescoes and mosaics.
Egyptian scenes became very fashionable.
This Pompeii mosaic depicts Nile wildlife.

MPEROR
his coin shows Philip
e Arab, another Roman
mperor who came from
ne of the provinces.
e was born in Syria and
igned from A.D. 244-249.

Family members
are wearing a
range of exotic
headgear.

Tunic and
trousers

EASTERN FAMILY

Roman provinces
often kept much
of their original
culture. This tomb
mosaic from Syria
shows an upper-class
family group. They
are wearing eastern-
style clothing and
they would have
spoken either in
Greek or Syriac.

Eastern slippers rather
than Roman sandals

LIFE IN ROME

ABOUT LIFE IN ROME

THE LIFE STYLE of an ancient Roman depended very much on income. The wealthy owned splendid houses with ornate decorations and had a staff of slaves to attend to every whim. These fortunate Romans wore fine clothes and ate sumptuous fare. At the other end of the scale, poor people lived in squalid accommodation and could afford only simple and basic food.

JEWELLERY
Wealthy Romans wore jewellery made from gold and precious gems. Poorer people settled for more modest items made from bronze or glass.

STREET SCENE
The streets of Roman towns were lively and crowded places, lined with every type of shop. Town-dwellers squeezed along the narrow pavements, rubbing shoulders with street vendors and musicians.

Reconstructed wooden balcony

Mud from the eruption of Vesuvius in A.D. 79 kept this Herculaneum building intact.

FEMALE SCHOLAR

EDUCATION
Women in Rome seldom got more than a basic education. Higher studies were strictly for the men, who were groomed for careers in the government. Poorer Romans, male or female, rarely received an education at all.

DECORATIONS

Houses often looked drab from the outside because the Romans were more interested in interior decoration. Inside, walls and floors were covered with paintings and mosaics. Elegant statues of gods, animals, or people stood in rooms and gardens.

COUNTRY PURSUITS

Many Romans lived in the countryside. The poor tended land rented from rich landowners and sold excess produce. The wealthy retreated to the countryside for holidays and engaged in pursuits such as hunting, seen in this relief.

LAMPLIGHT

Oil-burning lamps, made from pottery or bronze, provided the Romans with light. A large lamp might have 14 wicks.

LIVING IN ROME FACTS

• One million people lived in the city of Rome by A.D. 1.

• Romans washed up by scrubbing dishes with sand, then rinsing in water.

• Lead poisoning was common because of lead cooking utensils.

Boy removing thorn from foot

Hole for wick

BRONZE SCULPTURE

A TALE OF TWO CITIES

A GREAT TRAGEDY within the Roman empire left a treasure trove of priceless information. On 24 August, A.D. 79, near Naples in Italy, the long-dormant volcano Vesuvius erupted, burying towns around it in burning ash, stone, and pumice. After three days the sky cleared, but the two worst-hit towns, Pompeii and Herculaneum, were virtually forgotten for many centuries

PLINY THE YOUNGER
This scholar saw the eruption from across the Bay of Naples and recorded it in writing

MOUNT VESUVIUS ERUPTS
Everyone thought that Vesuvius was extinct. The mountain had not erupted for 800 years, and its tranquil slopes were covered in vineyards, farmhouses, and *villas*. During the eruption, ash and pumice blasted from the summit, landing up to 20 km (12 miles) away.

MAP OF DESTRUCTION
Straight after the eruption burning ash and pumice rained down on Pompeii. Only a little ash blew in Herculaneum's direction. But the next morning, surges of hot ash and gas and waves of boiling mud engulfed the entire town.

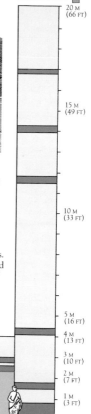

20 M (66 FT)

15 M (49 FT)

10 M (33 FT)

5 M (16 FT)
4 M (13 FT)
3 M (10 FT)
2 M (7 FT)
1 M (3 FT)

POMPEII SCENE

Today, the ruined streets of Pompeii still lie in the shadow of Vesuvius. On the day of the eruption, many of the town's 20,000 inhabitants escaped, running through the rain of ash. The next day, the 2,000 people who stayed all perished.

DEPTH OF ASH

The town of Pompeii was buried under 4 m (13 ft) of volcanic debris. Herculaneum was buried beneath 20 m (66 ft) of debris, the result of six surges of hot ash and gas and six mud flows.

Flow of hot ash, pumice, and rock

Surge of hot gas and ash

First, a rain of ash and stones buried Pompeii.

HERCULANEUM – OLD AND NEW

The new town of Herculaneum stands above the deeply buried Roman ruins. Vesuvius looms in the background.

Cities preserved

The abrupt burial of two towns allowed us to learn minute details about people's lives. Excavations began in the 18th century and, slowly, a picture of everyday life in both towns emerged. Pompeii was a thriving trading centre; Herculaneum was a fashionable seaside resort. Shops and bakeries lined the paved streets, and there were grand public buildings, such as theatres, temples, and bathhouses.

LOAF OF BREAD

PRESERVED EGGS

FOOD
Hot ash and gas turned the food to carbon. This loaf of bread, similar to modern Italian bread, was found in the oven of a Pompeii bakery.

Wet volcanic mud preserved bones but not body shape.

DOG MOSAIC
Many paintings and artefacts were preserved by the tragedy. This floor mosaic comes from a Pompeii entranceway. The dog was there to warn off trespassers.

HERCULANEUM SKELETON
In 1982, hundreds of skeletons were found in boat chambers in Herculaneum's ancient seawall. Before this, only a few bodies had been found in the town, and it had been believed that nearly everyone had escaped.

PLASTER CAST PROCESS
Ash and pumice set around the Pompeiians' bodies. When they decayed, hollow shapes remained in hard rock. Wet plaster was poured into the hollows.

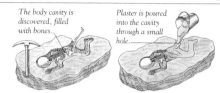

The body cavity is discovered, filled with bones.

Plaster is poured into the cavity through a small hole.

MOTHER AND CHILD
Here, a mother and child lie side by side, the mother trying to protect her offspring from the poisonous fumes.

Victim tries to shield face

Plaster cast preserves details

Casts show the Pompeiians in their death throes.

BABY
This suffocated baby was found in the area now called the Garden of the Fugitives.

MAN
This man was discovered crouching against the wall of the athletics stadium. He is trying to hide his face from the fumes. Most of those who died were suffocated.

LIVING IN TOWN

ROMAN TOWNS were bustling, noisy places. Only the privileged few could afford to live in a town house, or *domus*, a peaceful, private retreat that had no windows in the wall facing the road. By contrast, most people lived in apartment buildings, called *insulae*, with windows opening onto the streets and all their chaos.

Clay tiles, made from a mould

People ate while reclining on couches in the dining room, or triclinium.

Cheap rooms had no running water.

Walls facing the street were windowless.

The more affluent occupants lived in well-furnished, comfortable rooms.

The shops at the bottom created a lot of noise.

Balcony

Streets were dirty

A HOME IN AN APARTMENT BUILDING
A typical *insula* might have three or fou[r] storeys. The higher people lived, the worse the conditions were. On the ground floor the[re] were shops. First-floor apartments had several rooms. At the top, rooms were small and cramped.

Colonnaded garden

Many slaves were employed as maids, cooks, porters, and companions.

BEAUTIFUL TOWN HOUSE

Most Roman town houses followed the same plan. The *atrium*, or entrance hall, had a central opening in the roof to let in light. There was also an *impluvium*, a pool to catch rainwater. Various rooms led off the *atrium*. At the back was often a colonnaded garden, called a *peristyle*.

Bedroom

Mosaic floor

The family worshipped daily at the lararium, a shrine to the household gods.

Flushing toilets were connected to the town's sewers.

Impluvium

Guests were received in the atrium.

INSULAE AT OSTIA, NEAR ROME

These surviving *insulae* are solidly built of stone. *Insulae* were often made of flimsy wood and soared five storeys high. Overcrowding and ramshackle extensions caused frequent fires, and often whole buildings collapsed.

FURNITURE AND DECORATION

THE ROMANS had surprisingly little furniture in their homes. The lack of clutter made rooms appear elegant and airy, allowing full appreciation of exquisite statues and the fine paintings and mosaics that adorned floors, walls, and ceilings. A *domus* or *villa* might have beds, couches, cupboards tables, chairs, stools, and oil lamps. The rich spent a lot of money on marble, bronze, and rare inlaid woods.

DECORATIVE MOULDING
Intricate stucco reliefs, which blended with paintings and mosaics to form decorative panels, were a feature of many private houses.

Cupids harvesting grapes

WALL-PAINTING
The walls of luxury houses were painted with scenes that reflected every aspect of Roman life. This painting shows a group of women talking.

CAMEO VASE
This vase would have taken great skill to make. White glass was cut away over blue glass to make the pattern.

WALL MOSAIC DEPICTING NEPTUNE AND SALACIA

Mosaics covered many floors and walls. Skilled craftworkers worked from drawn plans, pressing tiny pieces of coloured glass or stone into wet plaster to make a picture or design. The subjects ranged from rural life to gods and goddesses.

TABLE LEG

...gs of tables were ...en ornamented ...th clawed or ...ofed feet. This ...g is from a three-...ged marble table.

Inlaid couch end

Stool

COUCH

One of the most important pieces of furniture was the couch. This was used for sleeping, eating, or simply reclining. Sometimes couches were high and had to be reached by a little stool. At dinner parties, a couch would accommodate three people lying side by side.

ROMAN CLOTHING

ROMAN FABRICS decayed long ago, but we know about the clothes people wore from paintings, statues, and carvings. Most clothing was made from wool or linen – luxury fabrics such as cotton or silk were expensive and had to be imported from India and China. The most common item of clothing was the tunic, a simple shift tied at the waist with a belt.

THE TOGA
Only citizens could wear the toga, a large piece of cloth wrapped around the body and flung over the shoulder. Togas were usually white. A senator wore a toga with a purple stripe.

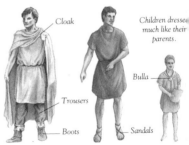

Cloak

Children dressed much like their parents.

Trousers

Bulla

Boots

Sandals

VARIOUS CLOTHING
Most poorer people wore just a tunic. In colder parts of the empire people wore woollen or felt cloaks, trousers, and warm leather boots. Boys wore *bullas*, childhood charms, around their nec

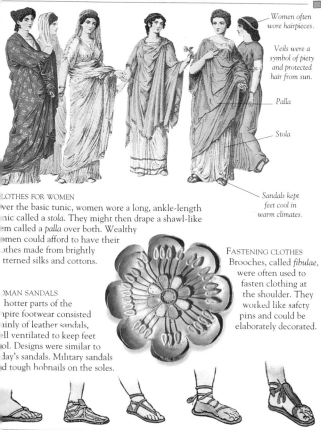

Women often wore hairpieces.

Veils were a symbol of piety and protected hair from sun.

Palla

Stola

Sandals kept feet cool in warm climates.

CLOTHES FOR WOMEN

Over the basic tunic, women wore a long, ankle-length tunic called a *stola*. They might then drape a shawl-like item called a *palla* over both. Wealthy women could afford to have their clothes made from brightly patterned silks and cottons.

ROMAN SANDALS

In hotter parts of the empire footwear consisted mainly of leather sandals, well ventilated to keep feet cool. Designs were similar to today's sandals. Military sandals had tough hobnails on the soles.

FASTENING CLOTHES

Brooches, called *fibulae*, were often used to fasten clothing at the shoulder. They worked like safety pins and could be elaborately decorated.

Jewellery and adornment

Roman men and women took care over their appearance. Men visited the barber for hair and beard trims; fashionable women, attended by slaves, performed a lengthy morning toilet of hairdressing and make-up. Men wore rings and fastened their cloaks with decorative brooches called *fibulae*; women draped themselves in necklaces, tiaras, bracelets, anklets, and earrings, fashioned from gold, silver, and bronze, often set with precious stones.

DOLPHIN EARRINGS
Roman earrings looked very like those people wear today. These gold earrings were made for pierced ears.

Mirror

Lock

VANITY CASE
Women kept jewellery and other valuables in special boxes. The box above also contains a mirror, cosmetic tools, and hair accessories.

ADORNED WOMAN
This Pompeii mosaic shows how a well-to-do lady might have adorned herself. Her carefully styled hair is tied back with a bandeau, and she is wearing jewellery and make-up.

PLAITED GOLD WIRE
NECKLACE WITH
CRESCENT-SHAPED
PENDANT

Hook fastener

Roman women
tinted their eyelids
with saffron
"eyeshadow".

RICH WOMAN'S JEWELLERY

The selection of jewellery shown
here would have belonged to a
wealthy woman. The pieces are
all made from gold and the
gemstones used would have
been gathered from territories
all around the empire. The
Romans also fashioned
jewellery from bits of glass,
polished up to imitate
genuine stones.

EARRINGS

GOLD NECKLACE
WITH RED
GARNET BEADS

MAKE-UP FOR ROMAN WOMEN
Pale skin was desirable, so white lead
was applied to the arms and face.
Cheeks and lips were reddened with
ochre. Antimony or black ashes went
on the eyebrows and around the eyes.

Ivory comb inscribed "Modestina, farewell"

HAIRDRESSING
Like today, hair fashions
came and went in the Roman world.
During the early Republic, beards for
men and a simple bun for women were
the style. Later, clean-shaven styles
for men and elaborate curls and plaits
for women were all the rage.

SHOPPING

IN ROMAN TOWNS, there were no supermarkets – people went to markets or specialist shops. These shops opened right onto the street. There were butchers, bakers, oil shops, wine shops, jewellers, and more. At the end of the day, owners shut up their shops by padlocking heavy wooden shutters to the pavement

The corn dole (free corn) was given out in the main hall.

Main street ran through the market

This terrace overlooked the forum.

Shops on ground floor were cooler

Staircase

MONEY AND COINAGE
At first, people paid for goods by bartering. Later, coins were made. During the Empire, most coins had the emperor's head on one side. The other side often publicized his successes.

OLD MALL
The empero
Trajan built
an enormou
shopping complex in Rom
It had 150 shops selling
luxury goods, such as spice
peppers, and silks from th
East, as well as ordinary far

A BAKER'S OVEN
Bakers' shops had
a mill at the back
where the flour was
ground. Dough was
made into round
flat loaves, marked
with the baker's
trademark, and
then baked in a big
oven, such as this
one from Pompeii.

STORAGE JARS
These pottery jars,
called *amphorae*, were
used to store and transport
oil, wine, and fish sauce.

STEELYARD
Traders used scales to weigh
a variety of goods. This type,
a steelyard, worked by hanging goods
from the hooks and moving a
weight along until it balanced.

...OK
...hold
...ods

...W OF SHOPS
...ops opened early and
...t late, with a break
...the afternoon. Some
...ps had signs outside
...vertising what was on
...e. Goods were often
...duced at the back of
... shop. Other goods
...ived by cart during
... night. Shopping
...eets were dirty
...d noisy places.

Workshop
making
scrolls for
writing

People lived
in rented
rooms above
the shops.

Bread was
baked in
ovens at
the back.

Butcher / Public fountain | Olive oil shop

IN THE KITCHEN

IT WAS QUITE A LUXURY to have a kitchen in Roman times. Poorer people, living in apartments, were lucky if they had a simple brazier or grill to cook on. Those who could afford to live in big houses had large, well-stocked kitchens, where industrious slaves prepared and cooked the meals. Many Roman kitchen utensils were similar to those used today, such as pots and pans, knives, sieves, ladles, and graters.

FOOD MOSAIC
Many mosaics depict food. These can give clues about what the Romans liked to eat.

MARCUS APICIUS
Apicius was a food expert. He devised many recipes – some of the strangest used nightingale tongues and camel heels! It is said he killed himself when he could no longer afford his taste for high living.

TAKE-AWAYS
Many poor Romans had no means of cooking their own food and were forced to go out to eat. They could eat in taverns or bars, or take food to the baker's and have it cooked for them in the oven. Take-away shops, called *thermopolia*, were especially popular. They served snacks kept hot in containers that were sunk into a counter.

Herbs were hung up to dry over the stove.

Game was hung before cooking.

Shelves held earthenware pots, dishes, and jugs.

The oil that was [stor]ed in amphorae [w]as used for both [coo]king and lighting.

Cookers were fuelled by wood or charcoal.

Kitchen floors were stone or decorated with rich mosaics.

ROMAN KITCHEN

This type of kitchen might have been found in a rich person's town house or country *villa*. Food was cooked in ovens or on top of charcoal on a stove. Food preparation centred around the table. Here, slaves would grind herbs and spices with a pestle and mortar, chop up meat and vegetables, and assemble eye-catching platters for dinner parties.

[NO] REFRIGERATORS
[Th]e Romans had [no] refrigerators, so [peri]shable food such [as f]ish and meat had [to b]e eaten promptly, [befo]re it went bad, [or b]e preserved by [pick]ling or salting.

FOOD AND EATING

THE ROMAN DIET included familiar ingredients such as meat, fish, and vegetables, though often combined in ways we might find odd today. Poor people existed mainly on a type of wheat and barley porridge, supplemented with vegetables – rarely meat. The first two meals of the day were

APPETIZER
Olives were popular as an appetizer. They would be followed by a glass of *mulsum* (honey wine).

often skipped. Dinner was the Romans' main meal, eaten in the afternoon. For the rich, this was a major gastronomic event that could last hours.

Celery

Mediterranean herbs and spices

FISHY FLAVOUR
Strong sauces, herbs, and spices were used to disguise the taste of meat or fish that had gone rancid. A sauce called *liquamen*, made from fish, salt, and herbs, was very popular.

PEACOCKS
The Romans ate exotic birds such as cranes, parrots, flamingoes, and peacocks. During lavish dinner parties, slaves would use the peacock feathers to fan their rich owners and brush away any flies.

Fish we kept aliv tanks fr eaten fr

pples, pears, grapes, figs, pomegranates,
tes, and plums were just some of the fruits
own across the empire. Many country estates
d orchards that supplied fruit to the towns.

*Fruit was
improved
by grafting
species.*

*Appearance was
important.*

INE
e Romans
nsumed a
at variety of
nes – sweet, dry,
d honeyed.
e wine was often
ong and heavy, so it was
xed with water in a special
xing bowl called a *cratera*.

*Decorative
relief*

MEDIUS				SUMMUS	
3	2	1	3	2	
				1	

I M U S	1
	2
	3

*The most prestigious
place to sit was at
medius 3.*

SEATING PLAN
At a formal dinner, three
ouches were arranged
round a square table,
eaving one side free for the
ervice. Each couch seated
three people. Social status
etermined where people sat.

ON THE MENU
Dinner consisted of three courses: *gustatio*
(appetizers such as salads and eggs), *primae
mensae* (up to seven dishes of meat, fish, and
poultry, such as the quail stew above), and, lastly,
secundae mensae (fruit, nuts, and honey cakes).

EDUCATION

ONLY FORTUNATE Roman children received
an education – many poorer children
had to work as soon as they were old
enough. Lessons consisted of learning
the basics – reading, writing, and
arithmetic. There was much chanting
of tables and learning by heart. From age
seven to 11 boys and girls attended the
primary school. Boys could then go on
to a grammar school, but girls had
to go home and
learn housework
in preparation
for marriage.

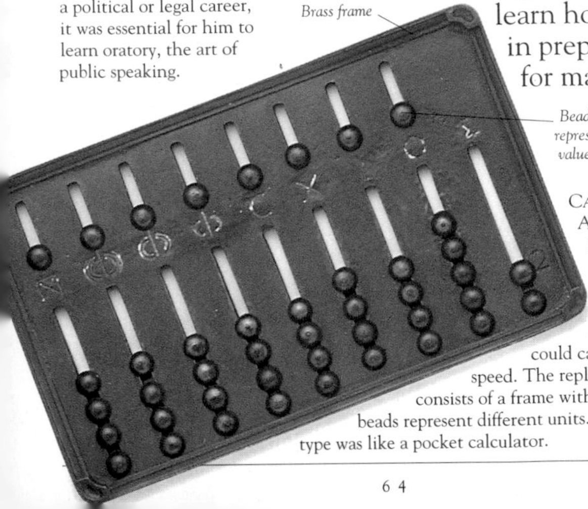

ORATORY
If a rich man's son wanted
a political or legal career,
it was essential for him to
learn oratory, the art of
public speaking.

Brass frame

Beads in upper part
represented five times
value of lower beads

CALCULATOR
An ancient
Roman used
an abacus
to help with
sums. An
experienced user
could calculate at great
speed. The replica shown here
consists of a frame with slots. Movable
beads represent different units. This compact
type was like a pocket calculator.

MAKING PAPYRUS PAPER

First, the outer rind of the reed was peeled off. The inner part was cut into strips, soaked in water, and placed in two layers – one at right angles to the other. The sheet was covered with linen and pressed with stones or a mallet. After drying it was polished and rolled up.

PEELED PAPYRUS

SLICED REED

STRIPS PRESSED INTO PAPER

WRITING SURFACES

Over 5,000 years ago, the ancient Egyptians discovered how to make a writing surface from the papyrus plant. Mostly the stem was used to make papyrus scrolls. Other surfaces the Romans used for writing were thin wooden tablets, bits of pottery, and parchment, made from animal skin.

Papyrus grew in abundance along the banks of the Nile.

WRITING

Children learned to write using stylus pens on wax tablets (wax in a wooden frame). Romans also wrote on papyrus sheets with reed or metal pens and ink made from soot. Here is a woman with pen and wax tablet. The man holds a papyrus scroll.

Cut stem

COUNTRY LIFE

FOOD AND GOODS produced by
farmworkers in the countryside
fuelled the great Roman towns. In
the beginning, there were numerous
small farmers eking out a modest
living. But by the time of the
Empire, much of the land had
been divided into great estates,
owned by wealthy Romans and
staffed by slaves. Landlords
spent much of the time in town,
using the profits from these huge farms
to finance their extravagant life styles.

HONEYBEE
There was
no sugar in ancient Rome,
so people sweetened food
and drinks with honey
collected from beehives.

EMMER WHEAT
Cereal crops such as emmer
wheat were grown in plenty.
Grain was made into
staple foods such as
bread or porridge.

COUNTRY PURSUITS
Hunting was a popular
country pursuit, both
for sport and to obtain
food. The quarries
included boar, hares,
deer, and game birds.
Horses and special
hunting dogs were
sometimes used.

AN OLIVE GROVE
Olive groves could be found in
many parts of the countryside.
Olives were eaten as fruit, but
the majority were crushed
in an olive press to extract
oil. The oil was stored in
amphorae and taken to shops
in towns or to ports for trading.

FRUIT AND VEGETABLES
Grapes were grown
both for eating
and for making
into wine. Typical
estates also contained
fruit trees as well as
vegetable gardens growing
crops such as radishes,
beans, cabbages, and
carrots. Potatoes
were unknown.

LIVESTOCK
The Romans reared various
animals on their farms.
Cattle and goats supplied
milk; oxen drew ploughs;
chickens, geese, and
ducks provided eggs;
and sheep were used
for milk, wool, and meat. Pork was
the most popular meat in ancient Rome.

A country estate

At the centre of the country estate was the *villa*, a luxurious country house. Inside, *villas* were beautifully decorated with mosaics, fine furniture, and paintings. Outside, there were well-tended gardens, fountains, and statues. Few *villas* existed without surrounding farms. These huge estates were self-sufficient, with everything from food and wine to bakeries and bathhouses. Usually, the day-to-day running of the estate would be the job of a farm manager, who oversaw a large staff of slaves.

FLOUR MILL
Many estates had their own bakeries. Donkeys or slaves turned the flour mills.

Store

Bakery

TRANSPORTING GOODS
Carts drawn by donkeys, mules, and oxen transported produce such as grapes, olives, and vegetables from outlying fields back to the estate.

Many types of fruit were grown in the orchards.

THE COUNTRY *VILLA*
There were three parts to the *villa*: the *villa urbana* was the luxurious part where the owner and family lived; the *villa rustica* housed the farm manager and labourers; and the *villa fructaria* was the storehouse for all the produce from the farm. The *villa urbana* had formal gardens to the front, and inside it was often arranged very much like a town *domus*.

Poultry provided eggs.

Shepherds tended sheep.

TREADING GRAPES AND MAKING WINE
Slaves picked grapes from the vines, loaded them
into baskets, and transported them to a special
stone trough. There, slaves crushed the grapes
with their bare feet. Great stone jars caught the
grape juice, where it would be left to ferment.

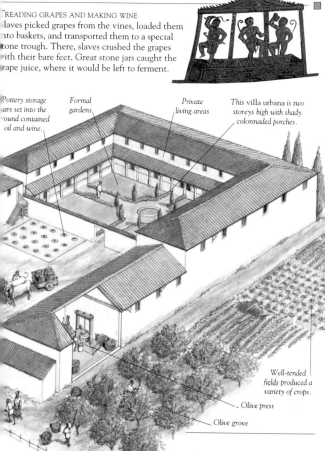

Pottery storage
jars set into the
ground contained
oil and wine.

Formal
gardens

Private
living areas

This villa urbana is two
storeys high with shady
colonnaded porches.

Well-tended
fields produced a
variety of crops.

Olive press

Olive grove

Hadrian's villa

Occasionally, *villas* were built purely as luxury retreats with no working farms attached. They were often near the seaside or not too far from towns. Emperor Hadrian built such a *villa* at Tivoli, near Rome. Built between A.D. 118 and 134, the *villa* extended over 120 hectares (300 acres) and contained buildings inspired by Hadrian's favourite sights from his travels around Greece and Egypt. In the grounds were bathhouses, theatres, libraries, temples, and accommodation for many guests and staff.

MARITIME THEATRE
The so-called Maritime Theatre is a round po[...] with an island in the middle, reached by a swing bridge. On the island was a pavilio[...] thought to be Hadrian's private studi[...]

Emperor's palace

Great bath

Canopus

Academy

Tree-lined walkway

Circular temple

Greek theatre

MODEL OF VILLA
This reconstruction show[...] how the *villa* would have looked in its heyday. The[...] buildings sprawled over a wide area, and the groun[...] were landscaped with sha[...] cypress-lined walkways a[...] sparkling fountains. Amo[...] many wonders was a cop[...] of the Grove of Academe[...] where Plato tutored stude[...]

BATH VAULTS

There were two bathhouses at Hadrian's *villa*. Each had several sets of rooms for steaming, massage, bathing in pools, or just resting. The ceiling vaulting on the baths is a fine example of Roman architectural skill.

EMPEROR HADRIAN

Born in A.D. 76, Hadrian ruled for 21 years. He was an intellectual with a passion for Greek culture. Hadrian spent much of his time travelling the provinces and visiting his armies and cultural centres such as Athens.

MPLE OF VENUS STATUE

ne central statue is a replica of
e 4th-century-B.C. original by
axiteles, a famous Greek sculptor.

HE CANOPUS

drian made an amazing replica of
nopus, an Egyptian town. He dug a
ge canal and imported Egyptian statues
decorate its banks. There were rows of
umns joined by alternate arches and graceful
yatids (female figures used as columns).

THE ROMAN ARMY

ABOUT THE ROMAN ARMY

MARCHING ACROSS THE WORLD and winning ever more lands for the empire, the Roman army was the key to Rome's success. In the early days, property-owning citizens left their farms and assembled into a part-time army during an emergency. Men supplied their own weapons. But as the frontiers of the empire widened, the army was reorganized and made permanent.

SOLDIERS OF THE REPUBLICAN ARMY
During the Republic, the army consisted of four types of soldiers. *Hastati* were young spearmen, *principes* were older, *triarii* were experienced and well armed, and *velites* (the skirmishers) were poor and lightly armed.

ARMY FACTS

• If a legion's "eagle" was captured in battle, the legion was disbanded.

• To stop enemy infiltration, each century had a password that was altered daily.

• Originally, only the rich joined the cavalry – they could afford horses.

• Hannibal's army lost 14,000 men and 25 elephants on its journey over the Alps.

PRIMA COHORS

LEGION

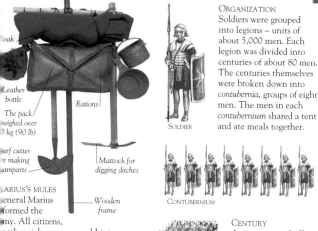

loak

Leather
bottle

*The pack
weighed over
kg (90 lb).*

Rations

urf cutter
r making
amparts

Mattock for
digging ditches

MARIUS'S MULES
eneral Marius
formed the
my. All citizens,
nether rich or poor, could join.
quipment and training improved.
oldiers were called Marius's mules
cause of their heavy backpacks.

Wooden
frame

SOLDIER

CONTUBERNIUM

CENTURY

ORGANIZATION
Soldiers were grouped
into legions – units of
about 5,000 men. Each
legion was divided into
centuries of about 80 men.
The centuries themselves
were broken down into
contubernia, groups of eight
men. The men in each
contubernium shared a tent
and ate meals together.

CENTURY
An experienced officer
was in charge of each
century. He had a special
crest on his helmet so his
troops could recognize him.

THE LEGION
A legion consisted of ten
cohorts. A cohort was a
group of centuries. The
first cohort, *prima cohors*,
was bigger than the rest,
consisting of ten centuries.
The other nine cohorts had
six centuries each. Every legion
carried a silver eagle standard,
which was a symbol of its power.

THE LIFE OF A LEGIONARY

HARDWORKING FOOT SOLDIERS called legionaries were at the heart of the Roman army. All legionaries were Roman citizens and joined up voluntarily, swearing an oath of allegiance. They underwent tough training to make the grade. Soldiers marched for miles, carrying heavy packs loaded with vital equipment – tools for building, pots for cooking, food and clothing. After 20-25 years of faithful service, soldiers were rewarded with money or a plot of land.

Ready to fire a stone

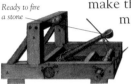

CATAPULT
The Romans often engaged in siege warfare. They surrounded an enemy and used battering rams and catapults to break down any defences.

A plume or crest could be attached to top of helmet

Neck protector

ARMOUR
This legionary's helmet was designed for full protection, shielding the head, cheeks, and neck without blocking out sound. A segmented metal jacket protected the chest area.

Cheek protector

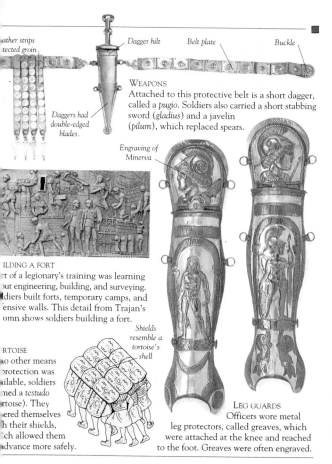

ather strips
tected groin

Dagger hilt

Belt plate

Buckle

WEAPONS

Attached to this protective belt is a short dagger,
called a *pugio*. Soldiers also carried a short stabbing
sword (*gladius*) and a javelin
(*pilum*), which replaced spears.

*Daggers had
double-edged
blades.*

*Engraving of
Minerva*

ILDING A FORT

t of a legionary's training was learning
ut engineering, building, and surveying.
diers built forts, temporary camps, and
ensive walls. This detail from Trajan's
umn shows soldiers building a fort.

RTOISE

o other means
rotection was
ilable, soldiers
med a *testudo*
rtoise). They
ered themselves
h their shields,
ch allowed them
dvance more safely.

*Shields
resemble a
tortoise's
shell*

LEG GUARDS

Officers wore metal
leg protectors, called greaves, which
were attached at the knee and reached
to the foot. Greaves were often engraved.

FOREIGN WARS

FROM THE BEGINNING, the
Romans fought wars. At
first they needed to defend
themselves from attackers.
Later they fought with othe
tribes in Italy to gain contro
of the whole country. Once th
was achieved, empire-building
began in earnest. Rome's army
fought on until it had conquere
a huge part of the known world

PYRRHIC WARS (280-275 B.C.)
This plate depicts a war elephant
used by King Pyrrhus of Epirus,
Greece, to fight the Romans for
Tarentum in the south of Italy.

BOUDICCA'S REVOLT
The Celtic queen
Boudicca led a revolt
against the Roman
army in Britain.
Despite some
success, she was
eventually defeated.

TRIUMPHAL ARCHES
The Romans erected
arches all over the
empire to celebrate
military victories.
This arch was built
in A.D. 26 at Orange
in Gaul, a territory
won by Julius Caesar.

PUNIC WARS
Between 264 and
146 B.C., the army
fought wars with
Carthage, in North
Africa. The skilled
Carthaginian general Hanniba
crossed the Alps into Italy with
elephants. After many battles,
Carthage finally lost to Rome.

TRAJAN'S COLUMN
By A.D. 100, Rome
had made most of its
foreign conquests.
But emperor Trajan
added Dacia to the
empire in A.D. 106,
and he built this
ornate column to
commemorate
his victory.

GAULISH ATTACK
In 390 B.C. the Gauls
attacked the city of
Rome. Only the
Capitoline hill
survived, saved by its
sacred geese that
warned of the attack.

When hired Numidian horsemen changed sides to Rome, Carthage lost.

Carthaginian standard

These spearmen were the only natives in the Carthaginian army.

Trained battle elephant

Spanish soldier hired by Carthage

A Roman soldier defends himself.

Fierce soldiers from Gaul wore patterned tunics and baggy trousers.

Celtic mercenary from Gaul

CIVIL WARS

THE ARMY did not fight wars just with foreigners. During Rome's long history, there were also many internal struggles when different factions of the army fought each other. During the time of the Republic, the main civil wars were caused when two strong leaders struggled for supreme power. This eventually led to the rule of the emperors.

Dagger with double-edged blade

Belt hook

Iron scabbard

PRAETORIAN GUARD
Emperor Augustus formed an army, called the Praetorian Guard, to protect him. Highly paid and very powerful, they murdered Caligula and, against the Senate's wishes, appointed Claudius (right) as the new emperor.

ASSASSINATION WEAPON
In 49 B.C., two powerful generals, Julius Casear and Pompey, were set against each other by the Senate. Caesar defeated Pompey and became Rome's sole ruler, but he was murdered by his enemies in 44 B.C.

FOUR EMPERORS (A.D. 69)

The year following the assassination of Nero was filled with conflicts and fighting. Four different emperors held power: Galba, Otho, Vitellius, and Vespasian (shown far left).

Slave

SLAVE REVOLT

In 73 B.C., a gladiator called Spartacus led a slave revolt, defeating two Roman armies. The revolt was crushed in 75 B.C., and 6,000 slaves were crucified.

0 km (100 miles) of crosses

Rome's Appian Way

OCTAVIAN V. ANTONY

Mark Antony and Julius Caesar's nephew Octavian became allies with the aim of avenging Caesar's death. But relations between the two men collapsed, and war broke out. In 31 B.C., Antony was defeated in a sea battle. This relief depicts a warship from the period.

81

BUILDING AND TECHNOLOGY

ABOUT BUILDING AND TECHNOLOGY

MANY ROMAN BRIDGES, roads, temples, and walls built 2,000 years ago still stand today. This is a testament to the skill of the Romans, who were also masters at copying good ideas. They borrowed building styles and learned about medicine from the Greeks.

NAILS
These nails would have been used in ship-building. Many Roman tools, such as chisels and squares, look the same as those used by builders today.

Inner sanctua

GREEK-STYLE TEMPLE
The Romans built Greek-style temple featuring a raised podium with colum that supported a triangular pediment

ANCIENT CRANE
This relief shows building in progress. The great wooden crane was driven by slaves walking a treadmill. Blocks of stone were tied to a pulley and the lifted by the action of the treadmill.

STURDY ARCHES

Arches had been built before, but the Romans built the most durable, using wood scaffolding to position stones or to lay concrete. Arches featured on aqueducts, theatres, amphitheatres, and bridges.

TECHNOLOGY FACTS

• People often secretly directed water pipes into their homes to avoid paying for water.

• Roman towns were built on a grid system.

• Quack Roman doctors prescribed gladiators' blood for fertility.

• A Roman mile was about 1,460 m (4,790 ft).

HEALING THE SICK

Although Roman doctors used a variety of science-based remedies to cure the sick, people often turned to the gods for help. After a devastating plague in the third century B.C., the Romans built this temple to the god of healing, Aesculapius. People left offerings at the temple in the hope of a cure.

DOME ON THE PANTHEON

The Romans invented the dome by crossing arches over a circular area. This magnificent dome was made with concrete – another Roman invention.

A hole at the top provides light.

WATERWORKS

ROMAN CITY DWELLERS NEEDED water in vast amounts for the baths, drinking, and lavatories. To bring this water to their towns, they built aqueducts all over the empire. "Aqueduct" means carrier of water, which is exactly what they did. Channelling water from rivers, lakes, and springs, aqueducts ran underground, through mountains, and across rivers and valleys to make sure the Romans got enough water.

ARCH OF DRUSUS
First mistaken for a triumphal arch, this is part of an aqueduct.

PINE CONE FOUNTAIN
Most Roman people had to collect their water from public fountains.

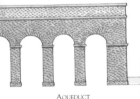

AQUEDUCT

RESERVOIR

PIPE

MAIN SEWER

AQUEDUCT IN ACTION
A water source had to be higher up than a town so gravity would ensure a flow. Water travelled through the aqueduct and collected in a huge reservoir. Pipes leaving the reservoir sent water to different areas, supplying public fountains, private houses (which were first to be cut off in a shortage), and the public baths. The waste ended up underground in the main sewer.

SEGOVIAN AQUEDUCT
This stone aqueduct in Segovia, Spain, was built in the early 2nd century A.D. and has 128 arches. Water was carried 30 m (98 ft) above the city along the top tier of the aqueduct.

PUBLIC LAVATORIES
Only rich households had the luxury of private facilities – most Romans used public lavatories like these. Water flowing past in a channel under the seats carried the waste away to the sewer. Like today, walls were often daubed with topical graffiti.

Only the wealthy had a private water supply.

PRIVATE HOUSE

PUBLIC BATHS AT CLUNY, FRANCE
Huge quantities of water were needed to run the baths, a popular part of Roman life throughout the empire. Doors usually opened at midday, announced by bells, gongs, or the shouting of slaves.

THE BATHS

PUBLIC FOUNTAINS

PUBLIC BUILDINGS

BUILT FROM FINE STONE such as marble, Rome's public buildings symbolized the empire's wealth and power.

At the heart of every Roman city was the forum, the site of government and business buildings. In addition to these were the bathhouses, temples, theatres, and amphitheatres that were such a key part of everyday life.

THE FORUM
Similar to a town square today, the forum was the site of markets and public meetings. Clustered around the forum were many public buildings.

TRIUMPHAL ARCH
Roman emperors built triumphal arches to celebrate military victories. The emperor Constantine built this arch in A.D. 315 to celebrate his victory over his co-emperor Maxentius.

Many reliefs and statues were taken from monuments of earlier emperors.

BASILICA OF CONSTANTINE AND MAXENTIUS

This huge 4th-century *basilica* was the last of the great public buildings to be erected in the Forum in Rome. Like all *basilicas*, it was used as law courts and for public functions.

Ceiling coffers were lined with marble.

The three barrel-vaulted aisles were used as law courts.

Constantine added main entrance in A.D. 313 after he defeated co-ruler Maxentius

The roof was supported by eight Corinthian columns.

TEMPLE RUIN
This temple from Rome's ruin was dedicated to Castor and Pollux, mythical twin sons of the god Zeus.

RECONSTRUCTION OF THE ROSTRA
The forum in Rome had a public speaking platform called a *rostra*. In 44 B.C., following the death of Julius Caesar, Mark Antony used this site to make his famous speech beginning, "Friends, Romans, countrymen, lend me your ears...".

Balustrade

Honorary statue

Panel relief depicts Trajan's acts of charity

The name rostra comes from the ships' prows, seized in a sea battle, that decorated it.

ROMAN ROADS

THE ROMAN EMPIRE was vast, so a good means of travelling across it was very important. The first roads were built for military reasons: the army built roads as they conquered new lands. Roads were built as straight as possible to help the army reach troubled areas quickly. Merchants later used these roads to transport goods.

ROMAN DRAINAGE
This drain was part of a system that prevented a city's streets from getting waterlogged. Roads also had sewage and water pipes running underneath them.

The surveyor used an instrument called a groma to check the road was straight.

BUILDING A ROAD
First the workmen dug a large trench in the ground. They put kerbstones on either side, then filled the trench with layers of stones, gravel, and sand. On top, they laid large paving stones. A surveyor made sure the road was level.

A camber (curved surface) drained off rainwater.

Layers were packed tightly together.

Kerb

IA APPIA

his famous road was the first link
a a network that eventually
overed over 96,500 km
50,000 miles). Named after
e censor Appius Claudius
aecus, who began it in
12 B.C., the Via Appia
onnected Rome to strategic
owns and ports in the south.

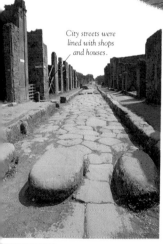

*City streets were
lined with shops
and houses.*

*Iron hobnails
positioned to
take soldier's
weight*

EPPING STONES

ads in towns had high pavements on
her side. When the roads were wet and
ddy, pedestrians used large stepping stones
cross to the other side. There were gaps
ween the stones for carts to drive through.

SOLDIER'S SANDALS

Each time the Roman army conquered
a new city, they had a road built to it.
Soldiers could march quickly along
these straight, hard roads. Military
sandals, called *caligae*, were strong,
well ventilated, and designed to
survive many long-distance marches.

TRANSPORT

GETTING FROM ONE PLACE to another in Rome was a lengthy business, even along its famous straight roads. Many people travelled by foot; others went in horse-drawn coaches or two-wheeled carts. Along the route were taverns and resting places, where a traveller could stay.

ON HORSEBACK
The official mail was relayed by horseback. Fresh horses were provided at resting houses (*mansiones*).

Milestones stood at the verges of roads and showed the number of miles still to go to reach a town.

FOUR-HORSE CHARIOT
Chariots were not just for the circus races. *Quadrigae* like this were used for ceremonial purposes such as processions to celebrate military victories.

CARRIED BY LITTER
Due to traffic congestion, carts were banned from the city of Rome during the day, so the rich travelled in litters carried by slaves.

HARBOUR SCENE
As trade increased around the empire, the Romans built deep harbours to serve the merchant ships that came and went. Rome was served by the port of Ostia, at the mouth of the River Tiber. These ports often grew into big towns.

Oar for steering

HORSE-DRAWN COACH
Like today's buses, coaches took a number of passengers on a journey. People sat both inside and on top. Coach journeys could be slow and uncomfortable.

Roman merchant ships had two masts.

Main sail

MERCHANT NAVY SHIP
Roman merchant ships had two masts and a hold for storing cargo. The ships were wide and sturdily built, able to transport large loads over vast distances. They could carry thousands of *amphorae* full of wine, oil, and fish sauce. Ships also transported wild animals for the arena, grain, cloth, gems, and spices.

Romulus and Remus, legendary founders of Rome

Steering sail

A lead coating prevented hull from rotting

Expertly joined planks of wood strengthened the hull.

HEALTH AND MEDICINE

ROMANS LEARNED what they knew about medicine from the Greeks. Doctors knew how to prepare soothing ointments and poultices for treating sores. They could also perform operations. But the average lifespan of a Roman was only about 40 years. Reasons for this included poor sanitation and epidemics of diseases that had no known cure.

GARLIC

FENUGREEK

MUSTARD

ELECAMPANE

FENNEL

This herb was used to settle the stomach.

SAGE

ROSEMARY

HERBAL REMEDIES
Doctors used many types of herbs and spices to make medicines. Infusions, taken internally, were made by mixing the herbs with warm water. Compresses, applied externally, were made by mashing herbs into a paste.

HEALING HERBS
Different herbs had different healing properties. For example, sage was thought to reduce fever, rosemary was prescribed for coughs, and garlic was fed to soldiers for health.

■

Curved tube
drained
bladder

SPECULUM FOR
INTERNAL
EXAMINATIONS

CATHETER

DOUBLE-
ENDED
HOOK

FORCEPS

*Squeezing
handles together
opened prongs*

SURGERY
With these
instruments
surgeons could
perform various
operations. But
as there were
no anaesthetics
in ancient Rome,
many people died
on the operating
table from the shock
and pain of being cut
open while awake.

EDICINE
SPOON

*Hook held back
sinews and veins*

ARMY DOCTOR
The only Roman
hospitals were army
hospitals, solely for
the treatment of
wounded soldiers.

*Army doctor
removes
arrow*

NGS
ople prayed to
e gods for cures.
ese rings depict
sculapius, the
eek god of healing,
d his daughter.

VOTIVE OFFERING
Sometimes people
had models made of
the afflicted parts of their
bodies. They left them in
temples when praying for
a cure, or else in gratitude if
the affliction had been cured.

GAMES AND
LEISURE

ABOUT GAMES AND LEISURE

WHEN IT CAME TO RELAXATION, the Romans were spoilt for choice. They could play games, go to the baths, or listen to music. The *ludi* (chariot racing, gladiatorial combats, and theatre) drew huge crowds. These were staged by emperors or senators in honour of a god or military victory. In reality, these lavish public entertainments were used as a way of winning popularity.

MUS
Roman orchestras, band
and solo musicians play
a variety of wind, string
and percussion instrumen
Here, the Greek god P
is shown playing a ly

AMPHITHEATRE
Gladiatorial games were staged all over the empire. This painting records a riot between Pompeiians and visiting Nucerians, in Pompeii to watch the games. An exchange of insults escalated, resulting in many deaths. Emperor Nero closed the amphitheatre for ten years as a penalty.

LEISURE FACTS
• Driverless chariots could still win a race.
• Playwright Terence was once a slave.
• Trajan held games lasting 117 days.
• 50,000 people died when an amphitheatre collapsed in A.D. 27.

THEATRICAL SCENERY

The theatre was so much a part of life that the Romans often used theatrical decorations in their homes. This wall-painting shows elaborate theatrical scenery. Going to the theatre (*ludi scaenici*) was a popular pastime, especially if a comedy was on the bill. If the audience became too rowdy, the producer called for silence.

BATH GAMES

The Romans liked nothing better than a trip to the baths for a good steam, scrub, and chat. The baths were also a place for playing games – ball games and athletics in the yard, or, for the less energetic, board-games or gambling in the shade, using dice like these.

COCKFIGHT

Many Roman leisure activities have endured to this day, including gruesome cockfights. Bets were placed and stakes were often high.

AT THE BATHS

MOST ROMAN TOWNS had at least one public bathhouse. The wealthy often had private baths in their homes. Public baths were not just places for washing – they were busy social centres, where people could exercise, chat, play games, do business, or even have their legs waxed.

Frigidarium
(cold room)

Tepidarium
(warm room)

BATH PLAN
The baths, like these at Aquae Sulis (Bath in England), consisted of a series of rooms, ranging from cold to very hot. Some had bathing pools or basins. The heat could be steamy, like a Turkish bath, or dry. On arrival, people undressed. They left their clothes in a changing room and then moved between the rooms, sweating, cooling off, and plunging into the pools.

Hypocaust

Laconicum
(hot, dry room)

Exercise ya *where peop* *wrestled, lift* *weights, o* *played gam*

Men and women went at separate times or had different bathhouses.

Carrying handle

Caldarium (hot, steamy room)

Implements attached by rings for easy removal

Hypocaust

Oil flask with detachable lid

The curved part of the strigil was used to scrape off dirt.

STRIGILS AND FLASK
The Romans did not have soap. Instead, they rubbed oil on their bodies, then scraped off the sweat, dirt, and oil with a *strigil*. At the baths, there were other health and beauty treatments available. These included massage, hairdressing, and several methods of hair removal.

TEPIDARIUM CHANGING ROOM
Inside, the baths were often lavishly decorated. The mosaic floor of this Herculaneum *tepidarium* shows Triton surrounded by dolphins.

HYPOCAUST SYSTEM
The floors, walls, and water were heated by a hypocaust system. An underground furnace sent hot air under floors and up through spaces behind special tiles on the walls. Floors were supported by spaced brick columns that allowed hot air to circulate easily. Water heated in a boiler above the furnace was sent to the baths through pipes.

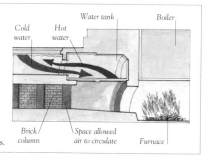

Cold water

Hot water

Water tank

Boiler

Brick column

Space allowed air to circulate

Furnace

PLAYING GAMES

THE ANCIENT ROMANS enjoyed games. Children's toys were not very different from those of today – they included dolls, model soldiers and animals, hoops and sticks, and marbles. At the baths, in the forum, and in taverns, adults played board-games with counters and gambled with dice. People of all ages enjoyed energetic ball games and athletics.

MINI CHARIOT
Only a child of wealthy parents would have had a toy like this mini goat-drawn chariot. Children's chariots were also pulled by dogs or geese.

GAMING COUNTERS
Counters had numbers, and sometimes names, on the back.

This means "worthless".

WINNING ATHLETE
Athletic contests were held in special stadiums. This athlete – probably a boxer – is holding a crown and a palm leaf, which was a symbol of victory.

Victory palm

WOMEN PLAYING
In this painting, the women are playing a dice game with knucklebones. Three knucklebones are on the ground and two are being thrown. Scores were kept for the different sides of the bones that landed face-upwards.

The size of the nuts is exaggerated in this relief.

GAME RELIEF
This relief shows children playing various throwing games. A game of nuts – marbles played with walnuts – is occupying most of the boys, although the two in the middle appear to have had a disagreement.

CHARIOT RACING

THE MOST POPULAR of the Roman games was chariot racing, or *ludi circenses*. Hordes of people gathered at the racetrack, called the circus, for a day out. Everyone had a favourite team, which they supported with the fervour of today's football fans.

In Rome, each team – the Reds, Blues, Greens, and Whites – had its own stables and trainers. Champion horses also had fans.

CHARIOTEER AND HORSE
This mosaic shows a champion charioteer from the Blues team. Although most charioteers were slaves, they could acquire great wealth and prestige. Fans knew a horse's pedigree and victories off by heart.

CIRCUS MAXIMUS
The Circus Maximus in Rome was the largest racetrack, holding 250,000 people. At the drop of a white cloth, the horses burst from the starting gates and thundered around the central island, or *spina*, finishing after seven laps.

TYPES OF CHARIOTS

This model shows a two-horse chariot, called a *biga*. Four-horse chariots, called *quadrigae*, were the most common. Charioteers tied the reins around their waists but carried knives so they were able to cut themselves free in the event of a crash.

Chariots were lightly built for speed.

Imperial box

AUDIENCE

All classes of Roman society enjoyed a trip to the races. The emperor and his family watched from the imperial box; others sat on tiered benches. Men and women could sit together, which made the races a popular place to meet people.

COLLISION

The most dangerous part of the race was at the turning points at either end of the central *spina*. This mosaic shows a collision. The confusion of limbs and wheels may well have meant death.

Horses were imported from the provinces, notably Spain and North Africa.

THE ARENA

THROUGHOUT THE EMPIRE people flocked to the *ludi munera* to see gladiators fight each other – and wild animals – to the death. At first, these fights were staged in the circus or in wooden arenas, but then special stone buildings, called amphitheatres, were built.

COLOSSEUM RUINS
Nearly two thousand years later, the ruins stand majestically in the centre of Rome.

The Colosseum

Of all the amphitheatres built to house the games, the Colosseum in Rome was the most spectacular. Commissioned by the emperor Vespasian, the Colosseum took ten years to build and was finally opened by the emperor Titus in A.D. 80. The 50,000 people it held could be evacuated in three minutes through the 80 *vomitoria* or exits.

NAVAL BATTLE
Built on the old site of Nero's artificial lake, the Colosseum could be flooded with water to stage mock sea battles. Gladiators fought each other from small ships.

Up to 100 ships
could take part

WILD ANIMAL FIGHT
Exotic animals were shipped in from all over the empire to fight in the arena. In games held by the emperor Trajan to celebrate his Dacian victory, 11,000 wild beasts perished.

106

Canopy stretched over top

Women sat high up.

The outside of the building was decorated with statues of gods.

STRUCTURE OF COLOSSEUM
The bulk of the Colosseum was supported by many arched vaults. People, carrying numbered tickets, entered through one of 80 ground-floor arches and then made their way along corridors and up staircases to their seats.

WINCHING UP
Beneath the floor of the arena was a network of corridors, cells, and machinery. Here, the animals were kept in cages. When the time to fight arrived, cages were winched up to arena level, and the animals were released through a trapdoor into the arena.

Gladiator, armed with spear, prepares to fight lion

Cage opened to allow animals to climb ramp to trapdoor

Cages were like three-sided lifts.

Slaves operated the winch to lift the cage.

Gladiators

The games lasted all day; anticipation mounted when the afternoon arrived. This was when the gladiators fought. "We who are about to die salute you!" they shouted to the emperor, and the fighting began. Gladiators were usually prisoners, slaves, or criminals. Some free men thought the gladiator's life was glamorous, and they volunteered, hoping for glory. Gladiators could train at special schools, where there were masseurs, doctors, and body-building foods.

COLOSSEUM GRAFFITI
Gladiators fought one-to-one, as shown in this graffiti. A heavily armed *secutor* (left) is pitched against a lightly armed *retiarius* (right).

Crested helmet made gladiator seem taller

The decorative reliefs that festooned a gladiator's helmet were often of gods and goddesses.

This bronze helmet, once polished and shiny, would have dazzled in the sun

Face guard was locked with twist-keys at front

HELMET
Gladiator armour was designed to look spectacular rather than help the wearer. This helmet's enclosed front would have given poor visibility. But, apart from perhaps arm and leg guards, this was the wearer's only protection.

Arm guard

Helmet flap to protect neck

…ulnerable
…as were left
…protected.

DIFFERENT TYPES
There were many types of gladiator.
A *retiarius* carried a net and a trident
and usually fought a *murmillo*, who wore
a fish-crowned helmet. *Thracians* had
round shields and curved daggers
and sometimes wore helmets.

RETIARIUS   MURMILLO   THRACIAN

GLADIATOR RELIEF
This relief shows two heavily armed
gladiators in combat. When wounded,
a gladiator could appeal to the crowd
for mercy. Thumbs up meant mercy
granted, thumbs down meant death.

WINNING GLADIATOR
Successful gladiators became stars. Many
victories could bring fame, fortune, and
freedom from slavery. Freed gladiators
often set up their own gladiator schools.

MUSIC AND DANCING

THE SOUND OF MUSIC rang through the Roman world. Music was played at the theatre, gladiatorial games, dinner parties, in the streets, and during funeral processions and religious ceremonies. Musicians were usually freedmen or slaves. The nobility often took music and dance lessons, but they never performed professionally, as this was considered vulgar.

Ornate handle

SISTRUM
This instrument worked like a rattle. The player held it by the handle and shook it, causing the bronze bars to jingle.

CORNU
Wind instruments were popular in ancient Rome. This long, curved horn, called a cornu, was sometimes used by the army for signalling.

TRAVELLING BAND
Bands of musicians travelled around and performed in the streets. This mosaic shows a child with a flute, a tambour player, and a dancer holding cymbals. The masked figure is playing double pipes – two pipes with reed mouthpieces, which were played simultaneously.

FUNERAL DANCERS
Dance was an important part of some religious ceremonies. This tomb painting shows the dance of the mourners – a group of women, wearing long, hooded cloaks, skip sideways, arms linked.

CONCERT
his wall-painting ows four women actising music for concert. A group e this, along with ncers, and perhaps robats, jugglers, and njurers, might well ve entertained nner party guests. e seated woman olaying a lyre. Its ings are plucked h fingers or a ctrum, causing e tortoise-shell ndbox to resonate.

Cymbals were often used in religious ceremonies.

Handle hold

ed together by chain

CYMBALS
Like their modern equivalent, these bronze cymbals were played by bashing them together. Cymbals were joined either by a rope, a piece of leather, or a chain.

THE THEATRE

THEATRE RUINS
The Romans built theatres all over the empire, like this theatre of Aspendus in Asia Minor.

THE ROMANS adopted the idea of theatre from the Greeks. At first, translations of Greek plays were performed. Later, original plays were written by Roman playwrights such as Plautus and Terence. Comedies were preferred to tragedies. Mime was a Roman invention, but, unlike today's mime, actors spoke!

IN THE WINGS
In this mosaic a group of actors are preparing for a play. Two actors are practising dance steps, one actor is being helped into his costume, and a musician is playing double pipes. Masks lie ready to be worn at the performance.

Poorer people sat higher up.

Underneath the seats, a network of corridors and stairs allowed easy exit.

THEATRE PLAN

oman theatre design followed that of
e Greeks, with some changes. Both
ere a D-shape, with tiers of seats. But
e seats in Roman theatres were often
pported by arches and vaults, rather
an cut into the slope of a hillside.
he first wooden theatres were later
placed by sturdier ones of stone.

MASKS

Theatres were very
big, so actors wore
masks to help the
audience recognize
the various types
of characters. Masks could denote
happy and tragic figures, male and
female, and young and old. Male
characters wore brown masks; females
wore white. Special devices were built
into the masks to help the
actors project their voices.

*The stone
background on
the stage was
elaborately
decorated.*

*A canvas
velarium could
be pulled over
these poles to
keep the sun off
the audience.*

*The orchestra
was the area
situated in front
of the stage.*

*The scenery could be
changed using special
machinery.*

*Hoists that lifted actors from the
stage, trapdoors, and other tricks
provided special effects.*

*A curtain fell to the
floor to reveal the stage.*

*Arches supported
the seats.*

RELIGION, FESTIVALS, AND DEATH

About religion, festivals, and death

THE ROMANS BELIEVED in gods, goddesses, and life after death. They adopted some of the Greek gods and merged the personalities of others with the existing Roman "state gods". There were also many lesser gods and spirits, and as the Romans conquered new lands they tended to absorb the new religions they encountered. Many festivals were held in honour of the gods.

GREEK GOD
Rome had no god similar to Greek Apollo, so they adopted him. He was god of the Sun and of prophecy. This is a Roman reproduction of a Greek statue.

ROMAN TEMPLES
Temples were built all over the empire and dedicated to different gods. They were also dedicated to emperors, who were often worshipped as gods. This temple in Rome, called the Pantheon, was built in honour of all the gods.

THE SACRIFICIAL ALTAR

At an altar outside the temple, offerings were made to the gods to keep them happy and to ask them for favours. Only priests could perform these complicated rituals because people believed the gods would not accept a sacrifice if a mistake was made.

Altar

SACRIFICE
Pigs, oxen, and many other animals died on the sacrificial altar during religious ceremonies. Animals were usually white, but black animals were offered to gods of the underworld.

FOREIGN GOD
Mithras was a Persian god, very popular with soldiers. Although the cult of Mithraism was in favour of equality, women were barred from joining the religion.

Bull's blood was held to be life-giving.

Mithras slays bull

THINKING ABOUT DEATH
This strange mosaic from Pompeii shows a skull with a measuring instrument. Its message is that death is a certainty, so life should be enjoyed, because death is the great leveller and gives a true measure of all things.

WORSHIP AND BELIEFS

THERE WERE NO CHURCH SERVICES in Rome – people took offerings to temples if they had a favour to ask a god. They also prayed daily at the household shrine. Worship consisted of processions, praying, and making sacrifices. During imperial times, many turned to foreign gods, who offered novelty and more involvement in religious ceremonies.

This temple was built in the 2nd century B.C.

GOOD AND BAD SIGNS
Romans set a lot of store by signs. Special priests examined animal innards or observed bird flight and cloud formation for omens. If sacred chickens ate hungrily, the gods were happy.

TEMPLE OF PORTUNUS, GOD OF RIVERS AND PORTS
Inside each Roman temple was a statue of the god or goddess to whom the temple was dedicated. People would visit the temple of their favourite god with offerings and pray privately for special needs.

CULT OF VESTA

Vesta was the Roman goddess of the hearth and household. Her shrine in Rome's forum was served by six women called the Vestal Virgins. Their task was to keep the shrine's sacred fire alight. They came from noble families and served Vesta for 30 years. The Vestal Virgins could not marry.

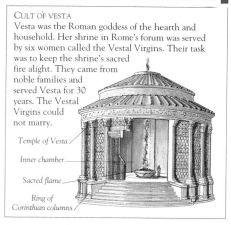

Temple of Vesta

Inner chamber

Sacred flame

Ring of Corinthian columns

WHICH GOD?

People would pray to different gods to ask for different favours. Venus was the goddess of love, beauty, and fertility.

MAKING A SACRIFICE

As the priest and his assistants performed the ritual sacrifice, a piper played a tune to drown any sounds of ill omen. The animal's internal organs were burned on the altar, and liquids such as wine were poured over to create a lot of smoke.

HOUSEHOLD GODS

Each house had a shrine, or *lararium*. The gods who looked after a house were called *lares* and *penates*.

GODS AND GODDESSES

THE ROMANS WORSHIPPED many gods and goddesses. These were seen as larger-than-life humans. They had their good and bad points, but unlike humans they lived forever. The state gods had the same personalities as their Greek counterparts but different names. Foreign gods were entirely different.

BACCHUS
This was the god of wine and revelry. His festivals were usually wild, drunken occasions.

Grapes, the symbol of wine

Mars was the Roman god of war.

Gilded silver

MARS ALATOR
The local gods of subject peoples often became merged with the Roman state gods. This temple offering from Britain was dedicated to a "mixed" god called Mars Alator.

CYBELE
A mother goddess and originally from Turkey, Cybele became part of the Roman state religion. These clamps may have had a gruesome use sometimes Cybele priests would castrate themselves for her.

Detail from triumphal arch

VICTORY
This winged figure personified success in battle. She often appeared on buildings erected to celebrate military victory.

Jupiter was god of the sky.

JUPITER
Known by the Romans as greatest and best, Jupiter was the king of the gods. His symbols were an eagle and a thunderbolt.

Anubis prepares body for afterlife

Busts of gods decorate clamps

Bronze handle

Head of a lion

JACKAL-HEADED ANUBIS
Anubis was the Egyptian god of mummification. Many people in Roman Egypt adopted Egyptian burial practices and were mummified after death.

FESTIVALS

ALL THROUGH THE YEAR the Romans celebrated many festivals. Most of them were religious, in honour of a certain god or goddess. Festivals were celebrated in a variety of ways. There were processions to the temple to offer up sacrifices. Festival goers also enjoyed eating, drinking, music and dancing, and lively public entertainments.

Vestal Virgin

1 MARCH
This was the day when the Vestal Virgins lit a new fire to the goddess Vesta at her shrine in the Roman forum.

SATURNALIA (7-14 DECEMBER)
The biggest festival of the year was held in honour of Saturn, god of agriculture. The Romans exchanged presents and gave dinner parties with a difference: masters waited on the slaves

FLORALES (28 APRIL–3 MAY)

This colourful festival was held in honour of Flora, the goddess of flowers. People wore garlands of fresh flowers on their heads and around their necks and celebrated by dancing.

Wild rose

PARENTALIA (13-21 FEBRUARY)

During this festival people honoured their dead parents. Temples closed down, and weddings were forbidden.

People visited the tombs of their parents.

JANUARY

On this day new consuls were sworn in at the Senate. Bulls were sacrificed to Jupiter to thank him for his protection during the past year.

SOME OTHER FESTIVALS

• 15 February – feast of the founding of Rome (*Lupercalia*): runners raced round Palatine hill, whipping spectators with goat skins.

• 15 March – festival of Anna Perenna: Romans picnicked by the Tiber.

• 13 August – feast of Diana, moon goddess: slaves had a day off.

DEATH AND BURIAL

THE RICH WERE TREATED very differently from the poor in death. A deceased noble lay in state in the *atrium*. A procession took the body through the streets on a litter, a speech was made, and a banquet held at the family tomb. The poor were often buried in common pits in public cemeteries.

Inscription says urn holds the remains of an "unfortunate mother"

BURIAL URNS

Cremation was popular for a long time in Rome. The ashes of the dead person were first washed with wine or water and then placed in an urn.

Glass urn

Marble urn

DIS MANIBVS
BOVIAE
PROC VLAE
MATRI MISERAE

Passers-by read inscriptions and remembered the dead.

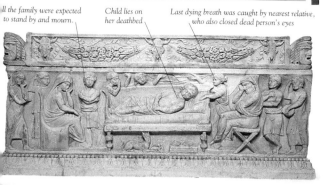

All the family were expected to stand by and mourn.

Child lies on her deathbed.

Last dying breath was caught by nearest relative, who also closed dead person's eyes

TRIP TO THE UNDERWORLD

Wealthy people could afford to have commemorative scenes (above) carved on their tombs. Most Romans believed that the dead were ferried across the River Styx to Hades (the underworld). Mourners would put a coin in the dead person's mouth to pay the ferryman.

Tombs like these once lined the Via Appia outside Rome.

Some tombs looked like miniature temples.

FUNERAL GAMES

The "games" in which gladiators fought each other to the death probably began as funeral games. Staged by nobles in honour of their dead relatives, these gladiatorial combats were looked on as a status symbol. The more flamboyant the show, the better this reflected on the host.

ROAD OF TOMBS

Burial grew popular in the 2nd century A.D. By law, bodies were buried beyond city limits – partly to stop disease. Tomb-lined roads existed outside most towns.

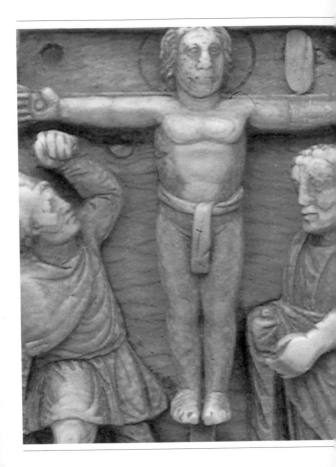

THE END OF
AN ERA

ABOUT THE END OF AN ERA 128

(COVERING THE DECLINE OF THE WEST
AND THE RISE OF THE EAST)

ABOUT THE END OF AN ERA

THE ROMAN EMPIRE ENJOYED PEACE and prosperity for over 200 years. But by the start of the 3rd century A.D. cracks were beginning to show. Such a large empire was difficult to manage and needed a strong leader. However, after the death of Marcus Aurelius (A.D. 180), there was conflict at the top, attacks on Rome's frontiers, and economic crisis.

This short, double-edged sword was a very effective stabbing weapon.

Baldric
(shoulder belt)

PERSECUTION OF CHRISTIANS
Many blamed Rome's demise on Christians, thinking they had angered the state gods by refusing to worship them. Roman Christians buried their dead in these underground chambers.

RULED BY THE SWORD
The death of Marcus Aurelius marked the beginning of a period when army generals fought each other for control. Over a span of 80 years, more than 40 different emperors came to power. Some only ruled a few months; many were killed.

Scabbard made from wood covered in leather and decorated in bronze

CLASPED HANDS

When two emperors co-ruled, this symbol often appeared on coins as propaganda to reassure people they got on.

BARBARIANS

Tribes known by the Romans as Barbarians began to attack the frontiers of the empire, especially along the Rhine and Danube rivers. The Romans allowed some to settle in the empire in return for their help in defending against any further invasion.

The Barbarians were skilled metalworkers.

Semi-precious stones

VISIGOTH BRONZE EAGLE-SHAPED BROOCH

CONVERSION TO CHRISTIANITY

In 312, emperor Constantine saw a flaming cross in the sky before he fought the usurper Maxentius for control of Rome. Constantine was convinced he owed his victory to God. This ended the persecution of Christians. Christianity was later to become the state religion.

The decline of the West

In A.D. 286 emperor Diocletian decided that the Roman empire was too big to be ruled by just one person. He appointed a co-emperor and two junior emperors. Diocletian ruled the eastern part of the empire, while his co-emperor, Maximian, ruled in the West. The East and West faced very different fates. Over the next 200 years the West steadily declined, until it had all but disappeared.

The Romans depicted death as a reminder to enjoy life.

Water pitcher

SKELETON MOSAIC

THE RICH GET RICHER

There had been a gradual polarization of wealth. While the rich gave lavish dinner parties, the poor could hardly afford to eat. Heavily taxed and stripped of many legal rights, the poor lost faith in the empire. Many preferred life under the barbarian invaders.

DEATH

Plagues raged through the western provinces, killing thousands of people. This meant that the empire had fewer workers, fewer slaves, and fewer soldiers.

Gesture of harmony

Egyptian coin

ECONOMIC DECLINE
Prices spiralled upwards. Between A.D. 200-280 the price of a bale of wheat in Egypt rose from 16 drachmas to 120,000 drachmas.

FARMERS
The cost of defending the empire was high and taxes were raised. Many farmers abandoned their farms because they could not afford to pay.

Farmers deserted their fields and became brigands.

Eagle symbolizes Roman empire

DIOCLETIAN
This emperor was a general, chosen by his army. He restored order and ensured the empire was run more efficiently, but his policies were very harsh. This statue, showing him, his co-ruler, and their two assistants as one, was meant to stress the unity of their rule.

The rise of the East

While the western half of the Roman empire declined, the eastern part of the empire flourished. Byzantium was rebuilt into the glittering city of Constantinople, replacing Rome as the capital of the empire. Out of the dying embers of the old, a new empire rose that was to last for another thousand years. Its people spoke Greek instead of Latin. We call it the Byzantine empire, named after the Greek city that was its birthplace.

CONSTANTINE
In 330 this emperor moved the empire's capital to Byzantium and renamed the city Constantinople.

THE ROMAN EMPIRE AT A.D. 330

VISIGOTHS SACK CITY OF ROME
Barbarian tribes had been allowed to penetrate the frontiers of the empire, and the Romans had become dependent on them for help with defence. But waves of attacks followed, and in 410 King Alaric of the Visigoths sacked Rome itself. It was the first time the city had been conquered for 800 years.

Barbarians used battleaxes.

THE END
The West survived for a time after the sack of Rome, but in 476 the last western emperor, Romulus Augustulus, was deposed by Odoacer, a German general.

central dome

Marble
and mosaic
interior

In 1453 the church
became a mosque.

Buildings were pillaged
and burned.

Visigoths rampaged
through the streets
for three days.

Christian King
Alaric ordered his
men not to steal
Christian objects.

Some Goths
had served as
auxiliaries in the
Roman army.

HAGIA SOPHIA (CHURCH OF HOLY WISDOM)

Eastern emperor Justinian (ruled 527-65)
reconquered lands that the Barbarians had
conquered in Africa, Italy, and Spain. He
also brought all the Roman laws together
in a book. In Constantinople he built
Hagia Sophia, which was the largest
church in the Christian world.

Cameo set in
ornately
worked
gold

BYZANTINE ART

Art, trade, and culture thrived in the new
Byzantine empire. Its capital Constantinople,
ideally located between Europe and Asia, grew
wealthy. Lavish mosaics decorated buildings,
and the rich wore jewels like this gold brooch.

REFERENCE
SECTION

THE GROWTH OF AN EMPIRE

THE VAST AREA known as the Roman empire was the result of many centuries of warfare. From a small city founded on the banks of the River Tiber in Italy, Rome grew into a powerful empire that stretched from the Atlantic Ocean in the west to the River Euphrates in the east, and from Hadrian's Wall in the north to the Sahara Desert in the south.

North Sea

LONDINIUM (LONDON)

Atlantic Ocean

NARBO (NARBON

TARRACO (TARRAGONA)

SEGOVIA (SEGOVIA)

CARTHAGO NOVA (CARTAGENA)

GADES (CADIZ)

Sahara Desert

AFRICA

PHASES OF EXPANSION
Rome's growth began with the gradual conquest of Italy. By the late 1st century B.C., Rome was ruler of every Mediterranean shore. The fall of Dacia (now Romania) in A.D. 106 brought the empire to its greatest extent.

EMPIRE AT 264 B.C.

EMPIRE AT 201 B.C.

EMPIRE AT 30 B.C.

EMPIRE AT A.D. 117

EUROPE

MARK OF THE EMPIRE
This inscription, which dates from the Republic, stands for *Senatus Populusque Romanus*, meaning "Senate and people of Rome".

Black Sea

ASIA MINOR

ROMA
(ROME)

POMPEII
(POMPEII)

BRUNDISIUM
(BRINDISI)

ALES
(IARI)

ACTIUM

EPHESUS
(EFES)

MYRA
(MYRA)

ANTIOCHIA
(ANTAKYA)

SYRACUSAE
(SIRACUSA)

CAESAREA
(SEDOT YAM)

RTHAGO
RTHAGE)

Mediterranean Sea

AELIA CAPITOLINA
(JERUSALEM)

BYZANTIUM
(ISTANBUL)

SABRATA
(SABRATHA)

LEPTIS MAGNA
(TRIPOLI)

CYRENE
(SHAHHAT)

ALEXANDRIA
(ALEXANDRIA)

Red Sea

ROMAN EMPERORS

THE CIVIL WARS that followed the death of Julius Caesar brought the period known as the Republic to an end.

Augustus	31 B.C.-A.D. 14
Tiberius	14-37 A.D.
Caligula (Gauis)	37-41
Claudius	41-54
Nero	54-68
Galba	68-69
Otho	69
Vitellius	69
Vespasian	69-79
Titus	79-81
Domitian	81-96
Nerva	96-98
Trajan	98-117
Hadrian	117-138
Antoninus Pius	138-161
Marcus Aurelius	161-180
Lucius Verus	161-169
Commodus	177-192
Pertinax	193
Didius Julianus	193
Septimius Severus	193-211
Caracalla	198-217
Geta	209-212
Macrinus	217-218
Elagabalus	218-222
Severus Alexander	222-235
Maximinus I	235-238
Gordian	238
Gordian II	238
Pupienus	238
Balbinus	238
Gordian III	238-244
Philip	244-249
Decius	249-251
Hostilian	251
Gallus	251-253
Aemilian	253
Valerian	253-260
Gallienus	253-268
Claudius II Gothicus	268-270
Quintillus	269-270
Aurelian	270-275
Tacitus	275-276
Florian	276
Probus	276-282
Carus	282-283
Carinus	283-285
Numerian (co-emperor)	283-284

Octavian, Caesar's adopted son, won the struggle for power. He restored normal government in 27 B.C. and was given the name Imperator Caesar Augustus. *Imperator* meant "victor in battle" and is the origin of the word emperor.

NOT A KING
Emperors wore wreaths of laurel rather than crowns.

GALLIC REBEL STATES	
Postumus	260-269
Victorinus	269-271
Tetricus	271-274

Weak emperors led to the creation of rebel states. The kingdom of Palmyra in the East and the "Gallic empire" of Gaul, Britain, and Spain were finally defeated by the emperor Aurelian.

EASTERN REBEL STATE OF PALMYRA	
Zenobia (Joint ruler with her son Vaballath)	266-272

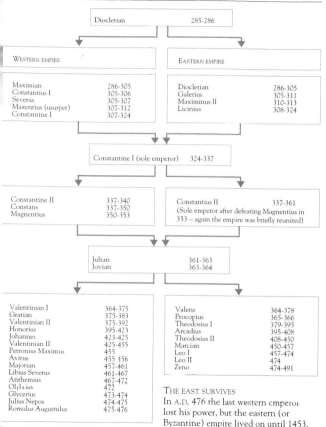

| Diocletian | 285-286 |

WESTERN EMPIRE		EASTERN EMPIRE	
Maximian	286-305	Diocletian	286-305
Constantius I	305-306	Galerius	305-311
Severus	305-307	Maximinus II	310-313
Maxentius (usurper)	307-312	Licinius	308-324
Constantine I	307-324		

| Constantine I (sole emperor) | 324-337 |

Constantine II	337-340	Constantius II	337-361
Constans	337-350	(Sole emperor after defeating Magnentius in	
Magnentius	350-353	353 – again the empire was briefly reunited)	

| Julian | 361-363 |
| Jovian | 363-364 |

Valentinian I	364-375	Valens	364-378
Gratian	375-383	Procopius	365-366
Valentinian II	375-392	Theodosius I	379-395
Honorius	395-423	Arcadius	395-408
Johannes	423-425	Theodosius II	408-450
Valentinian II	425-455	Marcian	450-457
Petronius Maximus	455	Leo I	457-474
Avitus	455 156	Leo II	474
Majorian	457-461	Zeno	474-491
Libius Severus	461-467		
Anthemius	467-472		
Olybrius	472		
Glycerius	473-474		
Julius Nepos	474-475		
Romulus Augustulus	475-476		

THE EAST SURVIVES

In A.D. 476 the last western emperor lost his power, but the eastern (or Byzantine) empire lived on until 1453.

ARCHITECTURE

MUCH OF ROMAN ARCHITECTURE was influenced by
the Greeks, but the Romans did make innovations of
their own. Massive arched aqueducts brought water to
the towns, where much of daily life was centred around
the fine public buildings of the forum, or town square.

DOMES

The dome was a feature of Roman
architecture that the Greeks never
employed. This construction was
a Roman invention. With its use,
together with arches and vaults,
the distinctive style of the interior
of Roman buildings began to evolve.

CROSS-SECTION
A domed roof is
constructed by
crossing a series
of arches over each
other, as this cross-
section shows.

PANTHEON

The most impressive example
of a dome is the Pantheon,
made possible by the
Roman invention
of concrete.

*Concrete cast with
hollowed panels
to reduce
weight*

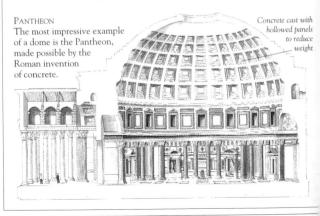

ARCHES

The use of the arch is a fundamental feature of Roman architecture. The Greeks and the Etruscans also built arches but did not use them in as many different ways. Before the Romans, most buildings were supported by columns and walls. Roman architects were able to build across greater distances because arches can support much heavier loads.

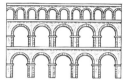

AQUEDUCTS

These consisted of a series of arches on several levels. The water channel at the top maintained a constant gradient.

THEATRES

The tiered seating in Roman theatres was supported by arches. The Greeks built their theatres on natural slopes.

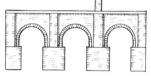

BRIDGES

Arched bridges could stretch across rivers and valleys. The hills on either side acted as buttresses, or supports.

TRIUMPHAL ARCHES

This type of arch had no practical function. The Romans built triumphal arches to celebrate victory in battle.

AMPHITHEATRES

Tiered arches supported the rows of seating, which completely encircled the amphitheatre's central arena.

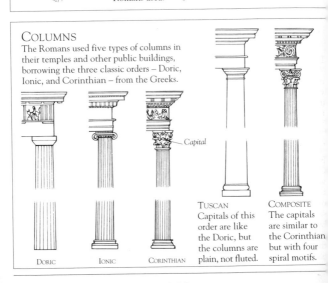

Vaults

These structures would have been difficult to build without the use of concrete. Vaults were built by placing a line of arches side by side to make a tunnel shape. Based on this model, different types of vault evolved.

Groin Vault
Crossing two barrel vaults at right-angles to each other formed the groin vault.

Barrel Vault
This tunnel-like structure was the original type the Romans used.

Ceiling
Groin vaults were first used in the Roman baths, as shown here in the Baths of Diocletian.

Columns

The Romans used five types of columns in their temples and other public buildings, borrowing the three classic orders – Doric, Ionic, and Corinthian – from the Greeks.

Capital

Doric

Ionic

Corinthian

Tuscan
Capitals of this order are like the Doric, but the columns are plain, not fluted.

Composite
The capitals are similar to the Corinthian but with four spiral motifs.

ORNAMENTATION

The Romans were very keen on decorating their public buildings with intricate motifs. Unlike the Greeks, who concentrated on exterior ornamentation, Roman buildings were just as lavishly decorated on the inside. Richly carved columns were often erected for decorative rather than structural purposes. Ornate friezes were another popular feature of Roman architecture.

ANTEFIX
A finial (bunch of foliage) design was often used as an antefix – a type of decoration that concealed the ends of roofing tiles.

ROSETTE
This rosette from the Forum of Nerva is made of acanthus leaves, a popular design and a characteristic of Corinthian capitals.

FRIEZE
This section from a Roman frieze depicts an entwined foliage design, which is then repeated. These decorative panels were also used to record events or tell a story.

CAPITAL
Ionic columns were decorated with twin spiral designs on either side of the capitals.

TEMPLES

Roman temples looked very like Greek ones – oblong in shape, with a triangular pediment over the entrance. There were usually rows of columns at the front and sides (a peristyle). Temples were built on a platform to make them stand out from other buildings in the town. A statue of the temple god was kept in an inner sanctuary.

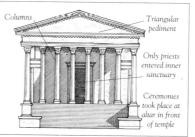

Columns

Triangular pediment

Only priests entered inner sanctuary

Ceremonies took place at altar in front of temple

TRADE

THE TRADING NETWORK of the Roman empire was vast and thriving. The provinces supplied Rome with a huge variety of goods; they also traded with each other. For a long time, there was peace throughout the lands and seas of the empire, so traders were safe to travel without fear of attack from bandits or pirates.

COMMODITY		ORIGIN (PRESENT-DAY LOCATION)
	Gold, silver, iron, copper, tin, lead	Spain had numerous mines. Britain, France, Cyprus, Turkey, and parts of central Europe exported metals.
	Fruit, fish, grain, salt	Egypt, Spain, N. Africa (main grain producers); Romania (salt); Mediterranean areas (fish and fruit).
	Honey	Greece was the main producer of honey within the empire. It was also imported from the Ukraine.
	Olive oil	The principal oil producers were Spain, N. Africa, Italy, Greece, Syria, and Turkey.
	Wine	Italy, Sicily, Spain, France, Turkey, the Greek Islands, and Syria were the main wine producers.
	Timber, marble	Greece, N. Africa, Turkey, Italy (marble); N. Africa, Lebanon, Turkey (timber).

Commodity		Origin (present-day location)
	Drugs, herbs	Egypt and N. Africa were the main exporters of drugs. Many herbs were grown in the Mediterranean regions.
	Purple dye	N. Africa, Israel, Lebanon, and Greece all produced this dye, which was distilled from murex seashells.
	Wool, textiles	Britain, Spain, Turkey, Syria, Greece, France, and Italy were exporters of these products.
	Glass, pottery	Greece, France, Germany, Spain, N. Africa, Turkey, and Italy all exported a range of these products.
	Horses, wild animals for the arena	Coastal towns in N. Africa and Egypt exported wild animals. Romania, Spain, and N. Africa supplied horses.
	Precious stones	Turkey exported emeralds. Most precious stones were imported into the empire from farther east.
	Leather, hides	These goods were mostly obtained from northern parts of the empire, such as Britain and the Danube lands.
	Ivory	Ivory was transported from central Africa and imported into the empire via the Red Sea.
	Papyrus	Papyrus grew in abundance along the banks of the River Nile. Egypt was the only exporter.

STATE RELIGION

THE ROMANS WORSHIPPED state gods and goddesses. This "family" of gods included husbands, wives, mothers, fathers, and children, who all had human characteristics such as jealousy. These Roman gods were very similar to the god family worshipped by the Greeks, and the Greek counterpart is given here in brackets after each Roman god's name.

JUNO (HERA)
Mother of war god Mars, Juno protected women, especially in childbirth.

JUPITER (ZEUS)
King of the gods, Jupiter controlled the skies and all celestial phenomena. Places struck by lightning were walled off and made his property. He married his sister Juno, but was forever unfaithful to her.

MINERVA (ATHENA)
She was the goddess of wisdom, crafts, and war.

AUGUSTUS
He was the first of many emperors to be deified.

DIS (PLUTO)
God of the underworld,
Dis was greatly feared.

NEPTUNE (POSEIDON)
The sea god rode a gold
chariot with white horses.

VESTA (HESTIA)
Bright and pure, she was
goddess of the hearth.

VENUS (APHRODITE)
Born from sea foam, she
was the goddess of love.

MARS (ARES)
This god of war was
the father of Romulus.

DIANA (ARTEMIS)
Moon and hunting deity,
her arrows brought plague.

APOLLO (APOLLO)
He was god of the Sun
and a patron of the arts.

MERCURY (HERMES)
This messenger of the gods
had winged sandals and hat.

BACCHUS (DIONYSUS)
Wine god Bacchus led a
band of merry revellers.

FAMOUS PEOPLE

THE ROMANS LEFT BEHIND a rich legacy in literature, language, architecture, and laws. Poets, writers, historians, political leaders, scientists, architects, and many others played a hand in shaping and preserving this legacy.

BOUDICCA (DIED A.D. 60)
Queen of the Iceni tribe in Roman Britain, Boudicca led a revolt against Roman rule in A.D. 60. The rebels wreaked havoc throughout eastern England and, according to Tacitus, killed 70,000 Romans and their British supporters. Britain's governor, Suetonius Paulinus, finally crushed the revolt. Boudicca probably killed herself.

CICERO (106-43 B.C.)
Marcus Tullius Cicero was a politician, scholar, lawyer, and writer. Educated in Rome and Greece, he became a great orator. Many of his speeches and writings have survived. He was in favour of the Republic and opposed Julius Caesar's dictatorship. He was later murdered for speaking out against the government.

CLEOPATRA (69-30 B.C.)
Cleopatra became queen of Egypt in 51 B.C. She was of Greek descent, but she spoke Egyptian and considered herself daughter of the Egyptian Sun god, Ra. Cleopatra was no beauty, but she did possess great charm, and she used this to seduce two great Romans: Julius Caesar and Mark Antony. This was probably more to enhance her power than for love. After Octavian defeated Antony at the Battle of Actium, both Antony and Cleopatra committed suicide.

COLUMELLA

Lucius Columella was born in Spain. He served as a tribune and fought in Syria. Columella was very interested in agriculture and wanted to find ways to improve production. In about A.D. 60 he wrote a set of farming textbooks in which he gave advice on *villas*, farm buildings, crops, and types of soil. His books were read avidly by many Roman landowners.

JUVENAL (c.A.D. 60-136)

This poet wrote about Roman life in works called satires. These are writings that criticize people's shortcomings and evils by poking fun at them. Juvenal attacked many things about life in the city, including the indiscretions of Roman society people and poor housing conditions. He described Rome as "a city that's propped up with little more than matchsticks".

LIVY (59 B.C.-A.D. 17)

Titus Livius, known to us as Livy, was a historian. He also tutored the young Claudius, future emperor. Livy's history of Rome, called "Books from the Founding of Rome", filled 142 books, but only 35 have survived. The history began at the dawn of Rome and was used as a textbook in Roman schools.

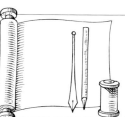

MARTIAL (c.A.D. 40-104)

Born in Spain, this poet liked to claim he was descended from Celts and Iberians. However, he was a freeborn Roman citizen and spent most of his life in Rome under the patronage of various aristocratic families. Martial invented the epigram, a type of poem with a witty ending. He wrote about everyday life and the leading individuals of Roman society.

PLAUTUS (c.254-184 B.C.)

This playwright wrote many plays, but only 21 have survived. Like other Roman dramatists, he based his plays on Greek comedies, but he introduced aspects of Roman life to make them more appealing to Roman audiences. Plautus influenced later writers, especially Shakespeare, who used Plautus's plots in some of his own plays.

PLINY THE ELDER (A.D. 23-79)

Admiral Pliny (as he was also known) commanded a fleet of warships. He died in the Vesuvius eruption when he sailed across the Bay of Naples in a bid to rescue trapped people. He wrote *Historiae Naturalis*, a natural history work in 37 volumes, which dealt with plant-based medicines, as well as anatomy.

PLINY THE YOUNGER (c.A.D. 61-113)

Gaius Pliny was eyewitness to the Vesuvius disaster that killed his uncle. Pliny the Younger trained as a lawyer. He served as a provincial governor, writing many letters to emperor Trajan. He also wrote to his friend Tacitus and others. His letters are full of information about events in the Roman world.

SENECA (c.4 B.C.-A.D. 65)

Seneca was born in Cordoba, Spain, but lived most of his life in Rome as a philosopher, poet, and lawyer. In A.D. 41 he was charged with adultery and banished to Corsica by emperor Claudius. He was later tutor and advisor to emperor Nero. Seneca retired because he was repulsed by the emperor's crimes. He was later accused of plotting against Nero and committed suicide.

SUETONIUS (c. A.D. 69-140)

Historian Gaius Suetonius Tranquillus was a friend of Pliny the Younger. He wrote several books. The most famous, called "Lives of the Twelve Caesars", is about Roman rulers from Julius Caesar to Domitian. It contains many scandalous and amusing anecdotes about these rulers' private lives.

TACITUS (c. A.D. 56-117)

Senator Cornelius Tacitus was a great Roman historian. His distinguished political career was probably aided by his marriage to General Agricola's daughter. He served as *proconsul* of Asia, the top provincial posting. His most famous published works are "The Histories" (the Roman empire from A.D. 69 to 96) and "The Annals" (A.D. 14-68: Rome's emperors from Tiberius to Nero).

VITRUVIUS (BORN c. 70 B.C.)

The architect and engineer Vitruvius wrote a guide for architects called "De Architectura", which covered different types of structures, like theatres and buildings in the forum. His guide also gave information on town planning and construction. Vitruvius was opposed to "modern" architecture, preferring the classic-style temples and public buildings.

ZENOBIA

Queen of the Roman colony of Palmyra in present-day Syria, Zenobia was not content with ruling under Roman control. She conquered Egypt in A.D. 269 and took most of Asia Minor in 270, declaring independence from Rome. Emperor Aurelian finally defeated Zenobia in 272 and took her to Rome, parading her in his triumphal procession. She went on to marry a senator and lived the rest of her life at their *villa* outside the city of Rome.

MUSEUMS AND SITES

THE FOLLOWING is only a partial list of museums and sites where ancient Roman artefacts and building remains can be seen. Many more exist throughout Europe, the Middle East, and North Africa.

Museums

UNITED KINGDOM

The Aldborough Roman Museum
Main Street
Aldborough YO5 9ES

British Museum
Great Russell Street
London WC1B 3DG

Chesterholm Museum
Bardon Mill
Hexham NE47 7JN

Colchester and Essex Museum
The Castle
Colchester CO1 1TJ

Corinium Museum
Park Street
Cirencester GL7 2BX

Museum of Classical Archaeology
Sidgwick Avenue
Cambridge CB3 9DA

Roman Palace and Museum
Salthill Road
Fishbourne
Chichester PO19 3QR

Royal Museum of Scotland
Queen Street
Edinburgh EH2 1JD

Verulamium Museum
St. Michael's
St. Albans AL3 4SW

Yorkshire Museum
Museum Gardens
York YO1 2DR

ITALY
Capitoline Museums
Capitol, Rome

National Archaeological Museum
Via Museo, Naples

The Vatican Museum
The Vatican, Rome

Sites

(Roman name shown in *italics* if different from modern name.)

UNITED KINGDOM
Arbeia Roman Fort
South Shields,
Tyne and Wear
Exhibits include personal items of Roman soldiers who served at the fort.

Bignor Roman Villa
Bignor, West Sussex
Includes some of the finest mosaics in Britain.

Caerleon Roman Fortress
Caerleon, Gwent
Includes barracks, an amphitheatre, and baths.

Hadrian's Wall
Northumberland
Roman wall that extends along the border of Scotland and England.

ullingstone
Roman Villa
ynsford, Dartford, Kent
Recreated Roman
ountry village.

The Lunt Roman Fort
aginton, nr Coventry
econstructed cavalry
ort showing the
rganization of the
oman army in Britain.

oman Baths
tall Street, Bath
Vell-preserved Roman
aths, with a museum
xhibiting offerings that
ere thrown into the
cred spring and many
her Roman artefacts.

oman Villa
ewport, Isle of Wight
xcavated villa with a
th and hypocaust
eating system, plus a
construced kitchen.

egontium Roman
rt Museum
aernarfon, Gwynedd
mous Roman outpost,
cluding a museum that
scribes the Roman
cupation of Wales.

Wroxeter Roman City
(*Viroconium*)
Wroxeter, Shropshire
Site of the fourth largest
town in Roman Britain.

FRANCE
Arles (*Arelate*), Provence
Remains of Roman city,
including amphitheatre.

Nîmes (*Nemausus*),
Provence
Remains of Roman city,
including the temple
"Maison Carrée" and a
famous amphitheatre.

Pont du Gard, near
Nîmes, Provence
Roman aqueduct.

GREECE
Athens (*Athenae*)
Remains of a Roman
arch, temple, odeon, and
other monuments.

ITALY
Herculaneum and
Pompeii, near Naples
Well preserved Roman
towns that were buried
when the volcano
Vesuvius erupted.

Rome (*Roma*)
The famous colosseum
and many other well-
preserved remains in this
capital of ancient Rome.

LEBANON
Heliopolis,
northeast Lebanon
Ruins of a temple
precinct, including the
Temple of Jupiter-Ba'al.

SPAIN
Alcantara, on the Tagus
River, near the border of
Spain and Portugal
Roman arch bridge.

Segovia, north of Madrid
Famous aqueduct.

TUNISIA
Dougga, southwest
of Carthage
Ancient Roman city,
including an impressive
temple and theatre.

TURKEY
Ephesus, south of Izmir
Extensive archaeological
remains of Roman town
life. Also, ruins of Greek
Temple of Artemis.

Glossary

AEDILE
One of four government officers in charge of public buildings, markets, and games.

AMPHITHEATRE
An oval-shaped theatre in which gladiator contests were held.

AMPHORA
A narrow-necked, two-handled vessel used for transporting and storing olive oil, wine, or fish sauce.

AQUEDUCT
Underground or raised channel built to bring water into towns.

ATRIUM
A house's central hall, onto which most of the rooms of the house opened.

BARBARIAN
Term the Romans used to describe anyone who lived outside the empire.

BASILICA
A large public building, usually located in the forum, which was used mainly as law courts or for ceremonies.

BULLA
A good-luck charm worn by a boy.

CENSOR
A government official elected to keep a record of all Roman citizens, issue contracts for roads and temples, and revise Senate membership.

CENTURY
A company in the Roman army consisting of 80 men, led by an officer called a *centurion*.

CIRCUS
Stadium where chariot races were held.

CITIZEN
Status granted to free-born men (first, to those living in Italy; later, to all provincials), giving them privileges such as the right to vote.

COHORT
A unit in the Roman army – there were six centuries in a cohort.

CONSUL
One of a pair of elected politicians that shared the highest position in the Roman government.

CONTUBERNIUM
The smallest Roman army unit, consisting of eight soldiers.

DICTATOR
A state official who was granted complete control by the Senate in times of crisis.

DOMUS
A private family home.

EMPEROR
The supreme ruler of all Roman territories.

EMPIRE
The Empire was the period in Rome's history (c.31 B.C.-A.D. 476) when Rome was ruled by emperors. The empire (without a capital letter in this book) describes all the territories ruled by Rome.

EQUESTRIAN
A wealthy social class descended from the first cavalry officers of the Roman army.

FORUM
Open area in a Roman town centre, used as a marketplace and to air public business.

GLADIATOR
A specially trained fighter who battled other gladiators to the death in amphitheatres throughout the empire.

HYPOCAUST
Roman-designed central heating system in which hot air created by a fire flowed through cavities under floors and in walls.

INSULA
A large apartment building of mainly rented accommodation.

LARARIUM
A shrine, found in every Roman home, dedicated to the worship of the household gods.

LEGION
The main division in the Roman army, consisting of ten cohorts.

LUDI
Term used to describe Roman entertainment, such as sports events, games, or theatre.

MOSAIC
A design or picture made with small pieces of stone, glass, or tile, usually cemented in a wall or floor.

ORATOR
A skilled public speaker.

PAPYRUS
An Egyptian water reed that was pressed out to make paper and then used for important Roman documents.

PLEBEIAN
A Roman citizen who was a member of the ordinary working class.

PRAETOR
A high-ranking, elected judge in the Roman state.

PRAETORIAN GUARD
An elite division of highly paid soldiers, founded by the emperor Augustus for protection.

PROCURATOR
Official in charge of looking after the finances in a province.

PROVINCIAL
A person who lived in one of the provinces governed by the Romans, but outside of Italy itself.

QUAESTOR
A government official elected to be responsible for the state's finances.

RELIEF
A carved or moulded picture that stands out from its background.

REPUBLIC
Period in Rome's history (c.509-31 B.C.) when the empire was governed by a system of elected representatives.

SENATE
A group of politicians that met to decide on affairs of state such as military matters.

SLAVE
An individual without rights who was owned by another and used for various types of work.

STUCCO
Decorative plasterwork on walls and ceilings.

THERMAE
A Roman public bath.

TOGA
Garment made from a (usually white) half-circle of cloth, which was draped around the body and worn on formal occasions.

TRIBUNE
A government representative elected by the plebeians to protect their interests.

VILLA
A wealthy family's country house, often on a farming estate.

Index

Acknowledgements

Dorling Kindersley would like to thank:
Hilary Bird for the index. Elise Bradbury
for editorial assistance. Carlton Hibbert,
Myfanwy Hancock, and Kate Eagar for
design assistance. Caroline Potts and
Robert Graham for picture research
assistance. James Mills-Hicks for
cartography. Henry Gewanter for the
Roman coins. Paul Roberts (British
Museum) for help with historical data.

Photographs by:
Peter Anderson, Peter Chadwick, Mike
Dunning, Steven Gorton, Christi Graham,
Frank Greenaway, Peter Hayman, John
Hesteltine, Dave King, Liz McAulay,
Andrew McRobb, David Murray, Nick
Nicholls, Steven Oliver, Kim Sayer, Karl
Shone, James Stevenson, Clive Streeter,
Matthew Ward.

Illustrations by:
David Ashby, Russell Barnett, Simone
Boni, Robin Carter, Steven Conlin,
John Davis, Peter Dennis, Paolo Donati,
Ray Grinaway, Kevin Jones Associates,
Thomas Keenes, Tony Morris,
Sarah Ponder, Sergio, John Temperton,
Peter Visscher, John Woodcock.

Picture credits: t = top b = bottom
c = centre l = left r = right
The publisher would like to thank the
following for their kind permission to
reproduce the photographs:

Ancient Art and Architecture Collection
21cr, 55b; Ashmolean Museum of Art
and Archeology, Oxford, 16tl, 133c;
Bridgeman Art Library 132bl / Galleria
degli Uffizi, Florence 19b / Musee
Crozatier, Le Puys en Velais, France 23t /
Musee Granet, Aix-en-Provence 146cl;
The British Museum 23c, 31b, 56t, 57t,
57c, 57bl, 65br, 94, 95tl, 95bl, 95bc, 101tr,
120bl, 120c, 120/121c, 121tc, 124, 125,
126/127; Capitoline Museum, Rome 19tr;
C.M. Dixon 129tr; E.T. Archive /
Archeological Museum, Naples 95br, /
Prenestino Museum, Rome 130 br; Mary
Evans Picture Library 46tr, 46c, 55t, 60c,
84c, 128cl; Werner Forman Archive 53bl;
Sonia Halliday 129bl; Simon James 1c,
21tl, 22/23, 30bl, 31tl, 36t, 39br, 40t, 40b,
45t, 51b, 66bl, 67bl, 74, 78b, 80r, 81b,
84bl, 93t, 96/97, 102c, 102/103b, 104,
105tl, 105b, 109t, 117bl, 123b, 131r,
jacket; The Mansell Collection 26r;
Museo Archeologico di Napoli 48tl, 48bl,
49cl, 49bl, 49r,130l; Museum of London
61t; University Museum of Newcastle 76b,
77;The Trustees of the National Museums
of Scotland 1995 2l, 5, 14tr, 39tr;
The Science Museum, London 3b, 58/59,
92/93, jacket; Tony Stone Images 12/13b;
Lin White 3cl, 14cl, 22bc, 32tl, 33b, 37tl,
37c, 41tr, 42/43, 44bl, 44cr, 47t, 47b, 52bl,
52br, 56br, 59t, 59c, 60b, 64t, 65bl, 87cl,
91cl, 92b, 98/99, 101tl, 103t, 108b, 110cl,
110b, 111, 112c, 113tr, 114/115, 117cl,
117cr, 119bl, 119br, 121br, 123cl, jacket;
Zefa Picture Library (UK) 87tl.

Every effort has been made to trace the copyright
holders and we apologise in advance for any
unintentional omissions. We would be pleased to
insert the appropriate acknowledgement in any
subsequent edition of this publication.